ASSOCIATION 4.0: POSITIONING FOR SUCCESS IN AN ERA OF DISRUPTION

Sherry Budziak and Kevin Ordonez

Cover designed by .orgCommunity, LLC

Sherry Budziak and Kevin Ordonez
Visit our website at www.PositioningForSuccessBook.com

Printed in the United States of America

Luminare Press
438 Charnelton St., Suite 101
Eugene, OR 97401
www.luminarepress.com

ISBN: 978-1-64388-006-8

Sherry Budziak and Kevin Ordonez

Sherry Budziak and Kevin Ordonez

CONTENTS

FOREWORD

I bet you didn't know that there is an association for bear research and management as well as one for Renaissance martial arts enthusiasts. The industries represented by trade and professional organizations are as diverse as human experience. But whether members make a living driving trucks, acting in movies or performing heart transplants, their expectations for education, information and advocacy are remarkably similar.

This is one of the many benefits of working in our unique economic niche. We can learn from the challenges and successes of organizations across the spectrum of business and apply those lessons to our own situation. The seventeen leadership profiles in this book represent a wealth of knowledge and experience. Regardless of the size or sophistication of the association you represent, you will become a better leader by exploring these professional landscapes.

As valuable as the collective wisdom in this book is, I'll issue a warning. You are about to venture into unknown territory. If you have been hiding from the future cloaked in the status quo, prepare for a reality check. The leaders who share their stories here are disrupters, innovators, and cultural shape-shifters. Some have had the courage to confront an untenable situation and accept the growing pains that were an inevitable component of success. Others have embraced change even though it came with professional risk.

Perhaps you and your board have been lucky. No crisis has rocked your industry or caused your members to question your mission. But If you imagine that clouds are not looming on the horizon, you simply have not looked far enough ahead. We are in the midst of a perfect technological storm. The same forces that are redesigning how business gets done are also reinventing customer expectations. Your members and constituents want you to deliver services and products better, faster and more personally than ever before. If your association can't meet those demands, trust me, someone else is waiting in the wings.

This book is both a wake-up call and a guide for navigating the future. If there is one overriding theme, it is that technology can no longer be regarded as a tool or a tactic. It must become a strategy that saturates every aspect of your business. My own experiences leading several associations through technological make-overs have convinced me of the truth behind this concept. In every case, the value derived from this approach far outweighed the effort. Digital transformation can give organizations the power and flexibility to move from mediocre performance to unqualified success.

The authors of this book are veterans in the technology space. They have seen it all—from faxes and modems to integrating CMSs, LMSs and CRMs. They are fearless trouble-shooters who have mastered diplomatic skills worthy of Middle East peace negotiators. But what has captured my admiration most is that as broad and deep as their expertise runs, they are still eager to discover the next new breakthrough or move on to the next platform. So, read this book! Enjoy the similarities and divergences from your professional environment and prepare yourself and your organization to break new ground, discover fresh markets and deliver the value your members will certainly expect.

Paul A. Markowski, CAE
Chief Executive Officer
American Association of Clinical Endocrinologists

Sherry Budziak and Kevin Ordonez

About the Authors

Sherry Budziak
Founder, .orgSource and Co-Founder, .orgCommunity

Most people who work for an association don't set out to have a career in the industry. My story is different. Ever since I was 14 years old, I wanted to work for a nonprofit. I discovered early how exciting it is to make a difference, and that thrill continues to inspire my personal and professional life.

At Valparaiso University, I was involved in AIDS awareness, date rape education, BACCHUS, Christmas in July, and many more philanthropic programs. My goal was to someday become an executive director and make a real impact in my community. At the time, a degree in nonprofit management was not offered, so I double majored in communications and political science.

The American Association of Neurological Surgeons/Congress of Neurological Surgeons (AANS/CNS), gave me my first chance to begin learning the ropes. David Martin, the assistant executive director at the time (now CEO at the Society for Critical Care Medicine), asked if I would help him create a website. In 1994, the internet was still largely uncharted territory, and we didn't have many examples to rely upon or inspire us. Although we took a lot of risks, in the end, we built an incredible online presence for the organization, which may have been one of the first association websites.

My experience with this new technology attracted interest from others. I was approached by the American Academy of Dermatology (AAD) to develop a for-profit subsidiary to help associations launch their online presence. It was an exciting and sometimes a scary challenge. My technology team and I survived the uncertainty of Y2K. We dealt with overheating server rooms and a host of other electronic nightmares.

Starting a business and selling to the association industry was a great adventure! As I advanced in the organization, I was once again asked to shoulder responsibilities for which I had no background. The executive director at the time, Tom Conway, CAE (now Chief Financial Officer at the American Association for Clinical Endocrinologists), appointed me to take on what had become his "IT headache." While it was more like a migraine, it gave me the experience I needed to start my consulting practice.

My career began with two association executives who took a chance on a young woman with more ambition than experience and the courage to try new things and take risks. The thrill of entrepreneurship—developing new products and revenue streams—led me to start a consultancy. For the last twenty-five years, we have supported associations with a wide range of services including strategic planning, technology, marketing and communications. Every day, I experience the value of my involvement with many organizations, their cultures and their management. My career has been an incredible journey. I am thankful to those from whom I have learned along the way. I look forward to helping others grow, lead and advance their missions!

Kevin Ordonez
Senior Consulting Partner, .orgSource and
Co-Founder, .orgCommunity

For as long as I can remember, I wanted to be a software and technology entrepreneur. Over the past quarter-century, I have had my share of challenges and success. With .orgCommunity, I am now on company number six.

During college, I joined the Association for Computing Machinery (ACM). There, I discovered firsthand the value of learning from peers, networking, and a feeling of belonging. At the ACM conferences, I met technological giants—people like Steve Jobs and Bill Gates.

After graduating from college with degrees in computer science and mathematics, I was fortunate to work for a consulting company in the Washington, D.C. area run by very a successful entrepreneur. My clients were among the most powerful trade associations in the country. I quickly noticed that adopting and leveraging technology was a common struggle. A few years later, I was hired by an association to help manage their technology infrastructure. As an "insider," I witnessed firsthand how far this organization was behind the curve. I realized that many other groups were also using outdated infrastructure, manual work-arounds and systems to track constituents, and experiencing an absence of innovation.

This was a big opportunity for an entrepreneur! I was inspired to start my first software company aimed at providing associations with better tools to manage their members, prospects and operations. Since then, I've had the ride of my life. I grew the company from three people with three computers in a basement to hundreds of staff in multiple locations around the country servicing thousands of organizations.

Even as a busy entrepreneur, I volunteered as much as my time allowed to the association industry. Over the last 20 years I have served on various committees and working groups as well as in leadership positions and on boards.

Experience has taught me that the most effective associations think like entrepreneurs and execute like Fortune 100 companies. There are several familiar mantras that reflect that concept. Here are a few of my favorites:

- What is your secret sauce? What do you offer that is uniquely yours?
- Get out of your comfort zone. Release creativity and innovation and welcome healthy debate.
- What is your TAM (total addressable market)? Think beyond "members."
- Don't be a "me too" organization. Focus on your business not your competition.
- A prospect is a prospect until they buy or die. Never give up on your prospects.
- Everyone is in sales. You, your volunteers, your staff, and even your detractors are out there selling for you (or against you).

The right leadership can transform associations, jumpstart their missions and create boundless opportunities. As Steve Jobs famously said, "The people who are crazy enough to think that they can change the world, are the ones who do.

Sherry Budziak and Kevin Ordonez

CHAPTER 1: ASSOCIATION 4.0 AUTHORS' PERSPECTIVE

"The Fourth Industrial Revolution is in its nascent stage but with the swift pace of change and disruption to society, the time to join is now."

—Gary Coleman, Global Industry and Senior Client Advisor, Deloitte Consulting.

This book represents both an end and a beginning. It is the culmination of experience gained over years of support to associations and their management. It is also the birth of what, we believe, will become exciting new strategies for keeping associations not just relevant, but thriving in an epoch of transformation.

One of the advantages of being a consultant is the opportunity to see how many different organizations approach similar problems. With a finger on the industry's pulse, we can recommend best practices, identify emerging trends and help our clients stay ahead of the curve. Over the last 25 years, technology has been front and center in our business. We have helped associations of every stripe organize and plan their technology functions and solve the sticky problems that come with the territory.

When we started out, IT was often an after-thought for clients, pushed to the back burner by more important priorities. In the blink of an eye, we've gone from bricks and mortar to carrying the world in our pockets. There is an app for everything from grocery shopping to picking stocks. Technology has invaded our lives with speed and rapacious zeal. We are connected to our possessions, our environment and each other in ways we could not have imagined fifteen years ago. IT departments, which once might have been a single misunderstood employee working in isolation, are now the nerve center of the organization.

We are standing at the precipice of an era that has been dubbed the Fourth Industrial Revolution—a time when the line between the physical, digital and biological will disappear. Current assumptions about the meaning of work, culture, and even humanity will be as altered as the world seen through Alice's looking glass.

The question is not whether to take the leap, it's how to survive the fall and the wildfire change that is certain to be a hallmark of this new era. Associations are whales, not dolphins. Turning on a dime is not in their DNA. Yet agility will be a requirement for the coming years, along with other shifts in attitude and behavior. For many association executives and boards, these new paradigms may feel as uncomfortable as the wrong size shoes until they are recognized as a mainstream approach.

Disruption is a buzz word that is often used to describe the cataclysmic changes that accompany advancing technology. It's easy to attach a negative connotation to break-throughs that are so revolutionary that they can vaporize an industry overnight and leave unemployed workers scratching their heads and wondering what happened. But it's important to remember that the flip side of disruption is creativity. You can make the choice to ride this precarious wave rather than letting it tow you under.

Our goal is to help your association outpace change and transform the accompanying disruption into success. We are passionate believers in the value of associations and the ability of their leaders to create organizations that will be as significant in the future as they are today.

DISCOVER ASSOCIATION 4.0

The Fourth Industrial Revolution signifies a new age for many industries. Association 4.0 is the name we've chosen to identify the leap our profession is about to make. As consultants, we have been acutely focused on identifying the shifts in attitude, culture and technology that are occurring and the most effective ways to navigate this unique environment.

The Innovation Lab is a think tank we created to explore these issues with association executives across a broad spectrum of the industry. The group meets on a regular basis to brainstorm and share their experiences. They discuss all things related to associations—from how to hire the best people, to how to recruit and orient board members and volunteers. Their objective is to analyze approaches that are effective and fearlessly confront patterns that need to change. The information gained in these forums has been used to create a new type of toolbox that associations can employ to strengthen their organizations and ensure success.

We also wanted to learn from leaders who are already being impacted by shifts in the sectors of the economy in which they operate. We surveyed more than 200 organizations and interviewed executives at 17 different associations. From movers of freight to movers of people, they represent a diverse group of membership organizations. Their stories, which form the basis for this book, illustrate challenges that are on the horizon and strategies for change and innovation that can be implemented to address unprecedented circumstances. Although the industries we write about may be very different from the business of your association, these examples can be viewed as a template for grappling with your group's complex issues and problems. You'll discover how:

- The American Trucking Association is handling a critical shortage of drivers and preparing for the advent of self-driving cars.
- The gurus of all things electronic at the Consumer Technology Foundation are educating policymakers to ensure that their innovation economy is protected from governmental restrictions that could hamper growth.
- Members of the American Planning Association are using big data to add a new level of certainty to urban planning.

As we compared these scenarios, common themes emerged. These concepts are fundamental to understanding and mastering Association 4.0. They represent overarching trends in our community as well as in employment practices that every leader will benefit from exploring.

BRACE FOR CHANGE

Imagine a time, in the not too distant future, when the world that once entertained or frightened you as science fiction is reality:

A Smartcar is driving you to your mother's house to wish her a happy birthday. You don't use the car often because for short trips the Transscoutter is a greener option and a lot more fun. When you're not with her, a Carebot is reminding your mother to take her medication and watching to make sure she doesn't trip and fall. Your mother's birthday gift is on the seat beside you. It's a personal 3D printer. It's incredibly easy to use, and your mom is going to have a great time printing up delicious desserts that are programmed to include her favorite flavors in a healthy format.

This personal scenario is playing out far more dramatically on the global stage. While the Carebot has enabled seniors to live more safely, robots have replaced thousands of human workers in every sector of the economy. Many people no longer have full-time jobs. Contract work is the norm rather than the exception. Technology has redesigned the landscape in ways that can't be described because the words to talk about these new developments have yet to be coined.

Even the most renowned futurists are shadow boxing at best. But tomorrow's needs and desires will certainly reflect technology's inescapable expansion. These are some assumptions that can be made about the impact of the Fourth Industrial Revolution on business and employment:

- Consumers will be impatient and exacting. They will want customized products and services delivered on demand.

  Imagine: Personalized, short mobile learning modules that use virtual and augmented reality based on recent knowledge gaps.

- A constant stream of customer data connected to smart devices will be available to continually upgrade products and services.

  Imagine: Trade show attendees receiving personalized follow-up after the show based on booths they visited and did not visit. And the association receives feedback on attendee traffic in real time with recommended changes to increase exhibitor exposure.

- Businesses will discover new structures for partnership and collaboration designed to deliver greater benefits to participants and to accelerate ongoing innovation in all their activities.

  Imagine: Contracts that include agreements and royalties related to ideas rather than products and services all stored on the blockchain, a highly secure public ledger system.

- Organizations that today seem unaligned will become indispensable to each other.

  Imagine: The American Heart Association and The International Society for Stem Cell Research collaborate to facilitate the development of new heart valves made from stem cells.

- Employees will be part of a global marketplace, giving them greater opportunity to specialize, to pick and choose assignments and to select nontraditional hours and workplaces.

  Imagine: Associations that have no permanent headquarters and few full-time employees and most of the work is performed by freelancers.

- Organizations will be more collaborative and project driven and less hierarchical.

  Imagine: Employees (or freelancers) being organized and led based on standalone projects rather than ongoing functions.

These are just a few of the threads that will intertwine as culture, work, production, and technology become more tightly woven together. No single phenomenon can be characterized as positive or negative. Each will come with huge benefits for some and hard consequences for others. The key will be understanding how to use the positive and avoid the negative aspects of each new development. This will require an unbiased attitude and the flexibility to accept and adapt to new circumstances.

UNDERSTAND THE PRICE OF INERTIA

While companies like Uber, Airbnb, and Amazon are harnessing technology to reinvent their industries, i.e. cause disruption, most associations are still plodding forward hobbled by Cretaceous era business models.

The way associations deliver products and services may have changed, but their organizational structures have not. They continue to be locked into bureaucratic, paternalistic systems that stifle innovation and, in some cases, actually prevent it from occurring. Acceptance of the status quo is entrenched in the culture. The willingness to change is overshadowed by the difficulty and risk involved in building something new. Along with advancing technology, there are other challenges on the horizon.

Competition

A short time ago, associations could easily identify their competition. Many groups were fortunate to be the sole occupants of their business arena. Today, your organization is surrounded by competitors and your members are bombarded by requests for their attention. A new online learning or communications group is born daily. Facebook, Twitter, LinkedIn and other social media offer multiple opportunities for networking and connection. There may even be for-profit groups that are seeking to seize a chunk of your market.

Demographics

The habits of millennials have been dissected, online and in print, as though they were some rare new species. But it bears repeating that this is a generation that has a very different perspective on belonging and volunteering. If the old association model is a bad fit for today's lifestyle and demographics, it is particularly unsuitable for this group. Younger people are looking for shorter, more impactful volunteer experiences that deliver an immediate return on their investment.

The dinosaurs, who reject change, have survived until now because the pace has been slow. But the asteroid that is going to wipe them out is hurtling toward us. Doing business as usual is no longer an option. This is an adapt-or-die situation.

POSITION FOR SUCCESS

Now, take a deep breath—because we are describing the near future—and think about *your* association. Ask yourself these questions:

- Why does our association exist?

  Consider what your members value about the work that you do. Rank these benefits in order of importance. Evaluate how your organization positively influences the profession and the public and rank these benefits by level of impact. Think about your visibility in your community, in the nation and on the international stage. How well are you recognized in each sector?

- If our association did not exist today, would industry leaders create it?

  Ask yourself whether the benefits you are providing are unique. Could your members receive these benefits elsewhere? If so, how deep is the duplication of services? How does the quality of your products stack up to others providing the same offerings? Assess your membership demographics. Are you consistently attracting new interest? Does your membership reflect the diversity of your industry? Does your leadership reflect the diversity of your membership?

- If not, why not?

  What circumstances have diminished the value your association can offer? List those conditions from most impactful to least impactful.

- In order to be relevant, how should your association's mission change over the next 10 years?

Consider what your organization can do to deliver new value to members. Think about what services, products and intangibles attracted members in the past and how those benefits could be updated to be meaningful in the future. Ask yourself whether you can extend the boundaries of your membership beyond your current constituent group. How can you broaden your scope to encompass a more global arena?

These are key questions that can be rigorously explored with your staff, your board and your members to assess your organization's strength and its ability to outpace change.

We've also identified attitudes that permeate the culture of the most successful associations and help them manage uncertainty in the outside environment. Effective leaders:

- Value professional development. They facilitate learning through formal education as well as through experience. They encourage employees to gain insights from one another and to respect their colleagues' expertise and professionalism.
- Foster creativity. New ideas are expected and welcomed.
- Promote a culture of innovation among the staff and board.
- Allow the freedom to act. Staff members are supported to make decisions and take risks.
- Are unafraid to acknowledge failure and learn from it.
- Invest in the technology they need to be successful and keep ahead of the electronic curve.

This adaptive mindset characterizes Association 4.0 thinking. It is the orientation that many of the executives we interviewed take towards their organizations. Courage is also an important ingredient in each of the stories you are about to read. The ability to leave what is comfortable behind in favor of a new and bolder vision, and to convince others to follow, is the hallmark of leadership.

Each story presents a unique perspective and offers lessons learned and food for thought. We've included our own ideas on the broad implications of these situations as well as questions for reflection and topics for dialogue. We hope that you will use these examples to begin having conversations with your board, staff, and volunteers that set the stage for a new beginning and position your organization to make the leap to Association 4.0.

CHAPTER 2: TAMING THE INFORMATION JUNGLE

Featuring: Peggy Winton, President and CEO, Association for Intelligent Information Management

Overview

Content that spreads like kudzu, data so camouflaged that it can never be found and compliance violations lurking in the swampy water—members of the Association for Intelligent Information Management (AIIM) are the experts who give systems as chaotic as the Costa Rican rain forest the order of an English garden.

AIIM, headed by CEO Peggy Winton, is waist deep in today's most ubiquitous business phenomenon—digital transformation. The organization provides research, education and certification programs to a global spectrum of information professionals. This up-to-the-minute orientation is the result of a long evolutionary process.

AIIM was founded in 1943 as the National Microfilm Association. As technology advanced, the organization's scope adapted and expanded with it. In 1982 the name was changed to the Association for Information and Image Management. By 2017 a new landscape was emerging. Technology, once a servant of many other business activities, had become the master of all. AIIM reinvented itself again. It kept its well-known acronym but adopted its current name to reflect a re-envisioned orientation and perspective. Although the organization runs ahead of the pack, it remains firmly focused on the long-standing goal of helping people put information to work.

AIIM by the Numbers

21 employees drive $5.5 million in annual revenue

155,000 active subscribers in dozens of countries worldwide

56% are from large enterprises

15% are senior management/executives

29% are from the line of business, 28% are IT staff, 26% are information professionals.

Top-5 regions represented: United States, Canada, United Kingdom, DACH, and Benelux

Top-5 industries represented: financial services (banking/insurance), government, healthcare/pharma, education, manufacturing/utilities and construction/engineering.

Sitting in the Crosshairs of Change

The industries represented by AIIM's members put them directly in the path of change and disruption. "Digital transformation has so many meanings," says Winton. "People are viewing technology and its relationship to their work in totally different ways. Change and new business models are occurring in unexpected places."

In this brave new world, where artificial intelligence and deep learning are redefining content management, AIIM had to consider whether its core services would become irrelevant. Leaders took a hard look at the technology landscape and their industry's competencies. They viewed their world through a kaleidoscope to see whether they could imagine it in a new way. That journey led them to the decision that content is, and will continue to be, a significant component of digital transformation. However, the board and staff also realized that this was the optimal time to define their purpose in more holistic terms and to move toward an analytic, data-centric, and application-oriented approach.

AIIM used information-driven terminology to develop a road map for digital transformation. The process, which they call intelligent information management, provides a foundation to support additional layers of resources and technology. AIIM now has a set of tasks and strategies that will integrate successfully with emerging trends. This approach keeps content relevant in the era of robotics and blockchain. The organization reinvented its industry practice and renamed itself to highlight this innovative approach to the future.

When an association makes such a significant leap some members bridge the gap more nimbly than others. Staff and volunteers may also need to recast their activities in a different light. As an example, Winton notes that among her constituents, compliance and records officers found themselves marginalized by business capabilities that bundled their services into larger platforms. As such, this segment of the membership needed to learn how to change the conversation about information governance. Instead of focusing on control, they discovered that they could flip the concept and highlight the value of using data to achieve exciting new business breakthroughs.

Seizing the UBER Mentality

Reinvention and renewal are entrenched in AIIM's culture. "Why" is a question that is always on the agenda. The organization constantly assesses operations to identify how to work better or smarter. "When you cast off old shackles, resources are freed up," Winton advises. "We're only 21 people, and we're driving $5.5 million in revenue. I'm proud of that. I think that is possible because we don't accept outdated models. I want my staff to be excited about working on innovative projects. When you remove the barriers, it's amazing what you can accomplish."

Winton believes that all associations can benefit from closer scrutiny of their intentions and purposes. She cautions, "Digital transformation isn't really about technology at all. It's about the need to anticipate and enhance the customer's experience. That's where associations fall short. We say that we are membership based, but are we really making it easier to do business with us? Are our products and services enriching people's lives?"

AIIM's culture makes customer satisfaction the driver of every initiative. In Winton's view, associations can't just meet expectations. They must be as good or better than other providers at satisfying their members' needs. Customized experiences at a click, from an array of dinner options ready to heat and eat to wardrobes selected by a personal stylist, are the norm rather than the exception. Association's that don't strive to meet their members' individual needs are flirting with irrelevance. Winton recommends seizing the Uber mentality to remove friction from everyday processes. "I challenged my team to make this the year of the hack," Winton said. "I urged them to figure out how to combine things that we already have in new and different ways."

In keeping with the philosophy of reinvention, AIIM long ago embraced an inclusive membership structure. "We saw the tremendous lifetime value of our relationship with people who, while consuming our extensive educational content and services, do not become dues payers. So many workers are now engaged in information management as part of jobs that have nothing to do with IT or records management. Enlisting them as subscribers gave us a revolving door of fresh new line of business owners who are today's ideal technology customers and a fantastic audience for the vendors in our space."

Growing New Leaders

A professional, as well as a personal, commitment to excellence defines Winton's leadership style. She is as focused on strengthening her team as she is on building a successful organization. "My personal goal is to make opportunities for the future leaders at AIIM. Our organization had been pretty tall and top-heavy. To change that, we came up with a structure that allows for on-demand project work in blended, cross-functional teams. It's a way to use people's best talents regardless of their department or responsibility." Winton also notes that this skill-based, collaborative model is the way millennials prefer to work. "The success is shared. Nobody feels like they have the entire profit and loss resting solely on their shoulders."

Helping other women succeed is an especially meaningful piece of Winton's professional development goals. She describes her vision like this, "I wanted to ask how women in this industry could better help each other. We launched a Women in Information subgroup to our community last year. We now have over 2,000 members who are actively involved. We didn't want it all to focus on technology or industry education. We really wanted to highlight helping other women achieve leadership roles within their organizations, on boards of directors, and within the AIIM community. I hope this will be a pipeline for our own board, and I view my younger staff in that same way. I want to create opportunities for them."

As she develops a leadership conduit to bring value to her organization, Winton also sees associations creating entirely new types of resources for their members and their industries' customers. Although the power of artificial intelligence and other emerging technology might make some uncomfortable (because of its human displacement potential), it can be harnessed to provide a deeper understanding of the business environment. Savvy leaders can use big data to identify all kinds of trends that lead to a deeper customer understanding. Winton also suggests that associations can heighten their consumer awareness by recruiting the younger generation. She says, "AIIM has 150,000 subscribers. We are capturing and analyzing so much behavioral information that we can use in a variety of ways to enhance the customer experience both for our members and ourselves. In the near future, when we are able to add the power of AI to our data analytics, we will have an incredible resource that we can use to create engagement that becomes increasingly meaningful and rewarding for our constituents."

What Association Executives Can Learn From AIIM

1. Confront disruption creatively. AIIM prepared for the future by closely examining its purposes and determining how to repackage its mission.
2. Question everything. Winton and her team are not afraid to ask "why?" They objectively evaluate procedures and processes and eliminate outdated activities that no longer serve their customers or their mission.
3. Seize the UBER mentality. Winton challenges the staff to think creatively. They actively seek to combine existing components in exciting new ways.
4. Create opportunities for leadership. Winton believes that when you elevate your team, you strengthen your organization.
5. Be a big tent. Recruit younger people for your team and be diverse. Insight from many perspectives generates ideas and innovation.
6. Consider a more fluid organizational structure. Cross-functional teams play to employees' skills and interests. This approach encourages creativity and initiative.
7. See opportunity over challenge. Identify hard trends, then apply the power of new technology to better understand customers.

Food for Thought

- Could your association's mission be viewed in new and more creative ways?
- Are you questioning your procedures and policies frequently enough?
- Are there outdated activities and systems you could shelve to make room for new initiatives?
- Could your association benefit from a more fluid organizational structure that includes blended cross-functional teams?

CHAPTER 3:
INTELLECTUAL CAPITAL EXPANDS MEMBERSHIP AND GENERATES REVENUE

Featuring: Irv Bomberger, Former Executive Director, American Orthopaedic Society for Sports Medicine

Overview

When an Olympic superstar crashes in the half-pipe or wipes out on the slopes, specialists in sports medicine are called on to do the meticulous job of putting broken bones back in working order. Members of the American Orthopaedic Society for Sports Medicine (AOSSM) get injured athletes on their feet and back in the game.

AOSSM represents orthopaedic surgeons in the United States and internationally who specialize in sports medicine. The organization offers world-class education, research and fellowship in this medical subspecialty. The group collaborates with many other providers and clinicians who treat athletic injuries. Family physicians and emergency physicians, pediatricians, athletic trainers and physical therapists are among the caregivers who partner to improve the identification, prevention, and treatment of sports injuries.

Established in 1972 primarily as a forum for education and research, AOSSM has grown from its modest initial membership of fewer than 100 to more than 3,000. Through advances in research and surgical and rehabilitation techniques, orthopaedic sports medicine specialists can successfully treat athletes whose injuries were once career ending. AOSSM members are unified in their concern regarding the impact of athletic activity on individuals of all ages, abilities, and levels of competition. They must demonstrate continuing research and educational activities in the field. Involvement could include serving as a team physician at any level of competition, educating providers about the health of athletes, participating in local, regional, national and international competitions, and presenting scientific research papers at sports medicine meetings.

AOSSM by the Numbers:

- More than 3,400 national and international members
- Doubled in membership since 2002
- 83 percent of AOSSM members are team physicians
- Approximately 75 percent of AOSSM members' practices are devoted to sports medicine
- 46 years of representing the orthopaedic profession within the sports medicine community
- $2.6 million in funding for clinical and basic science research grants since 2005, with an average grant of $65,000

The AOSSM Advantage: Reading Its Customers

When Irv Bomberger was asked about his proudest accomplishment during his 20-year tenure at AOSSM, he unequivocally states it is AOSSM's development and growth as a publisher of outstanding research and educational periodicals. He believes journalism is the key to AOSSM's future success and a path that other associations serving medical subspecialties should consider modeling.

AOSSM's monthly journal, *The American Journal of Sports Medicine* (*AJSM*), is a top-rated, peer-reviewed publication of scientific research that includes articles on basic science and clinical topics. In 1986, *AJSM* was self-published, "but over time we realized this wasn't our forte," Bomberger says. In 2004, AOSSM transitioned the management and production of *AJSM* to SAGE Publishing, the world's fifth largest journal publishing company, with a portfolio of more than 1,000 journals in the humanities, social sciences, science, technology and medical fields. AOSSM maintained ownership as well as editorial control and oversight. SAGE dramatically increased journal revenue and modestly increased subscriptions from slightly more than 8,000 to nearly 9,400 during a period when many journals experienced a decline in subscribers.

In 2002, AOSSM launched a digital version of *AJSM*. This decision both maintained the level of subscribers and increased their diversity. More importantly, digitizing *AJSM* made it more widely accessible through institutional consortia, which also helped to grow its impact factor (the yearly number of citations to recent articles published). *AJSM*'s five-year impact factor is number 1 out of 74 orthopaedic journals and number 5 of 82 sport sciences journals, according to 2016 data (http://journals.sagepub.com/impact-factor/ajs). More than 8 million readers each year access the journal online, with publication downloads averaging 1.3 million. "While subscriber volume stayed roughly the same, the journal's usage went up dramatically," Bomberger says. The journal's online usage is approximately 900 times greater than its subscription volume.

Launching an iPad mobile app version of *AJSM* seemed like the next logical iteration for the journal, which occurred in 2013. Surprisingly, the app hasn't received much traction. "Only a fraction of the subscribers (5 percent) use it," Bomberger says. "We found that readers access the journal's various platforms— print, online, mobile app—differently depending on their needs. For instance, younger readers use their phones to look up information on the fly, but they turn to their computers for searching and downloading more robust research that might be challenging on mobile devices." Younger members also still read the paper version of the journal or even print PDFs of the articles that they find important. The organization concluded that the different publishing platforms enhance the usefulness of *AJSM*'s content by allowing subscribers to access information in the most convenient formats. Bomberger believes it is a dangerous decision to opt only for print or digital publication of a journal. While the iPad app has had only nominal use up to this point, he believes that format for publication is still evolving.

By 2009, *AJSM* was successful enough to warrant embarking on a second journal. *Sports Health: A Multidisciplinary Approach*, offers a distinctive clinical focus that extends beyond orthopaedic surgeons to include topics of interest to all medical professionals involved in the training and care of athletes. Primary care physicians, physical therapists, and athletic trainers are among the intended audience. Published bimonthly, *Sports Health* is a collaboration with the American Medical Society for Sports Medicine, the National Athletic Trainers' Association, and the Sports Physical Therapy Section. The periodical is provided as a benefit to their respective memberships and to institutional subscribers such as universities, hospitals and professional practices. It publishes review articles; original research on treatments and techniques; case studies; special reports on imaging, nutrition, legal issues and other topics; as well as editorials. In seven years, *Sports Health* has built a subscriber base of 25,000—2.5 times that of *AJSM*.

Subsequently, AOSSM began investigating whether to launch an open access journal. The opportunity surfaced when AOSSM realized many quality articles rejected by *AJSM*, because of its limited capacity, were appearing in other publications and achieving high citation rates in the broader orthopaedic sports medicine community. "With the journal having a 75 to 80 percent article rejection rate, and those rejected manuscripts having the benefit of *AJSM*'s rigorous peer-review process showing up elsewhere, it was time for a paradigm shift," Bomberger says. The *Orthopaedic Journal of Sports Medicine* (*OJSM*) was created in May 2013 and introduced a new publishing option to the field of orthopaedic sports medicine. *OJSM* is an open access journal, meaning the content is available to everyone online, without charge.

Because it is an electronic publication, there are no printing costs. The savings in space and dollars allow the Society to publish a higher volume of articles, which also can be longer and easily include full data sets and video features. While *OJSM* still emphasizes high-quality, peer-reviewed research, it does not need to limit what it publishes to only those manuscripts deemed to be the most significant scientifically.

However, the cost of maintaining a high-quality peer review and editorial process, as well as providing a robust digital publishing platform and servers, cannot be offset only by digital advertising. Therefore, AOSSM, like all open access publishers, charges authors an article processing fee. The cost is lower for authors who are members of *OJSM*'s 19 international co-sponsoring societies. Processing fees are waived for authors from certain developing countries.

"The article processing fee can be the Achilles heel of open access journals if they are perceived as a 'pay-to-play' publication," Bomberger says. But the editorial board—with members from more than 30 different countries—is intent on maintaining a high level of scientific rigor, he adds. "Content is still peer-reviewed by a minimum of two reviewers and an editor to ensure its integrity. The open access model enables AOSSM to appeal to a truly international constituency of authors and readers, collaborate with other societies, and connect with other organizations. In this way, AOSSM is using publishing to attract intellectual capital. It serves a very good purpose."

OJSM publishes an extensive variety of works, including original research, systematic reviews, and meta-analyses. The fields of orthopaedic sports medicine, arthroscopic surgery, sports epidemiology, knee arthroplasty and others doing clinically relevant foundational and translational research are represented.

After four years, *OJSM* is now close to breaking even, and article downloads and citations have surpassed expectations.

"We have always asked which publishing model will win out—subscription or open access," Bomberger says. "In actuality, all of AOSSM's publishing models enhance each other."

Building Knowledge Equals Bolstering Future Success

Bomberger believes it's imperative that associations remain a trusted source of information to safeguard their survival. To continue their value to members and customers, associations must increase the education they provide and build their bodies of knowledge.

"Intellectual capital is really the strength of an organization, not just its financial resources," Bomberger says. "Increasing your volume of knowledge through education and published content will help medical specialties and subspecialties thrive and survive."

Bomberger is convinced, "Growth is not just the number of practitioners, it's advancing the body of knowledge and, therefore, advancing science. If the science grows, the number of clinicians and members will grow."

What Association Executives Can Learn From AOSSM

1. Continue to read your customers. You facilitate the growth of a profession by providing respected, authoritative and widely accessed content in your field that meets information needs.
2. Know when to engage outside help. AOSSM realized it wasn't proficient at self-publishing *The American Journal of Sports Medicine*, so it outsourced the management of it to SAGE Publishing in 2004.
3. Cast a wider net. Collaborate with other allied groups to expand your knowledge offerings and gain more members, like AOSSM did when launching *Sports Health*.
4. Experiment with new models. These can either complement or enhance existing formats, such as what AOSSM did with launching its open access journal in 2013, *Orthopaedic Journal of Sports Medicine*. Explore opportunities to eliminate cost barriers and increase speed to market, as well as increase non-dues revenues.

5. Remain a trusted source of information by attracting new intellectual capital. Continually develop your bodies of knowledge with original research to advance the profession, and the members will come.
6. Maintain your integrity. A higher volume of knowledge cannot come at the expense of integrity.

Food for Thought

- What is your association doing to increase your members' professional body of knowledge?
- Are you producing products/information that is of interest to people outside your membership?
- How could you expand the audience for your publications?
- Are you offering publications in all the formats that are convenient for your members?
- Have you done the research to understand your audience and learn how they want to receive information?

CHAPTER 4: CITY PLANNERS OUTRUN TECHNOLOGY'S TIDE

Featuring: Jim Drinan, J.D., Chief Executive Officer, American Planning Association

Overview

City planners are the set designers of our daily lives. They are the architects of the spaces in which we live, work and play, Planners may have an impact on the transportation you take to your job, the location of your favorite park, or the preservation of historic buildings in your neighborhood.

The American Planning Association (APA) is the organization that advances the work of these professionals who manage the development of urban landscapes. According to the APA, "Planners help government officials, business leaders, and citizens create communities that offer better choices of where and how people work and live." This is a multidisciplinary field that includes specializations in:

- Community Development
- Land Use and Code Enforcement
- Transportation Planning
- Environmental/Natural Resources Planning
- Economic Development
- Urban Design
- Planning Management/Finance
- Housing
- Parks and Recreation
- Historic Preservation

- Community Activism/Empowerment

Planning, which is inextricably tied to technology, has a profound impact on the social, cultural, economic, and environmental future of communities. In their role as the arbitrators of public spaces, planners must possess the ability to convene officials and citizens and bring them to consensus around decisions that enhance the sustainability of the neighborhoods, towns, and cities they serve.

City planners have been organized in the United States since 1909 when the first National Conference was held in Washington, D.C. Twenty-five years later, its sponsor, the American Society of Planning Officials, was incorporated. In the interim period, the American City Planning Institute was incorporated in 1917. For 44 years, these organizations coexisted until they merged to form the APA in 1978.

Today, the APA provides leadership in the development of vital communities by advocating excellence in planning, promoting education and citizen empowerment, and providing members with the tools and support necessary to meet the challenges of growth and change. It also operates the American Institute of Certified Planners (AICP), the only nationwide, independent verification of planners' qualifications.

APA by the Numbers:

- 35,000 members from 100+ countries
- 47 chapters throughout the United States
- 21 divisions that embrace the wide range of planning
- Two office locations: Chicago and Washington, D.C.
- 2015 total assets: $18.1 million

Navigating Policy, Technology and the Future

A focus on the public good and the underlying principles that support it contributes to one of this profession's core strengths. Planners can bring diverse groups of people together in productive conversation. They arrive at common ground, sometimes under the most difficult circumstances, by emphasizing policy over politics. Increasingly, data also play a role in achieving consensus.

Today, the ability to mine big data brings a level of certainty to planning that helps to ensure success and provides an evidence-basis for decision making.

Information from numerous different sources can be gathered and analyzed to answer important questions such as what the best location for essential city services is.

As an example of this trend, APA CEO Jim Drinan notes that to determine where to locate a police station or health care facility, planners might look back over the last 100 years to identify patterns in the calls for emergency vehicles. They would review and analyze historic and current information to identify the most efficient placement for these critical services.

Planners also use scientific research to emphasize facts over faction and deflect politically charged conversations. A paper or journal article about temperature patterns and sea level changes in coastal cities could provide the basis for a compelling argument with global warming naysayers. Of course, this means that the planner must also be well-prepared for the conversation and speak with authority on a topic that may be outside their primary expertise.

Big data is just one of several technology trends that are front and center in the planning arena, according to Drinan. The race to develop the first commercially available self-driving car promises to also have planners working overtime, considering the impact of these vehicles on urban spaces and their residents.

"The reduction of drivers is not just a professional issue; it is a social issue," Drinan says.

The American Trucking Association reports that there are more than 3.5 million truck drivers in the United States. If truck drivers and others in the transportation workforce are displaced, communities will experience the effects of unemployment and revenue loss as well as a concurrent increase in social services that provide job retraining.

Cars aren't the only vehicles creating disruption in urban spaces. Planners are also wrestling with how drones will affect air rights, privacy, insurance, and zoning.

While technology complicates the playing field, it also provides planners with increasingly sophisticated tools to help them do their jobs. Augmented reality devices developed by Oculus, Microsoft, and Google can support collaboration between teams and computers by superimposing 3D images into physical space. These holograms can be manipulated by team members working together to make planning decisions. This technology has the potential to change the way city planning is accomplished. Drinan notes, "Planners will be able to ask questions such as, What happens if instead of the building being this tall, it is that tall? What happens if it's this shape, not that shape? What is the impact of the sunlight? Are people likely to walk on the sidewalk or not? There is a lot of really cool stuff on the way."

Reaping the benefits of technology while mitigating undesirable consequences will be the challenge of planners for years to come. That is why—regardless of age, level, role or specialization—understanding and embracing technology is a professional imperative. Drinan says, "You have to. You can't say, 'Okay, you're the millennial, you learn how this thing works.' Every planner needs to know how [relevant technology] works to make thoughtful, informed and strategic decisions on behalf of their constituents—now and in the future. Emerging technology is just one more field of expertise planners will be required to develop to be successful."

What Association Executives Can Learn From Planners

1. Understand and build expertise in related fields. Planners must become experts on potentially any topic impacting their work. For example, planners who specialize in transportation must understand the engineering behind building a train line. They need to be aware of alternative transportation options, such as electric buses, and to quickly acquire and assimilate knowledge. Likewise, association professionals need to be adept at understanding the total environment in which they operate and how innovation and disruption will impact their ability to achieve their goals and their mission.

2. Collaborate upstream and downstream. New developments, such as autonomous vehicles, may have a positive impact on the supply chain, but city planners must take a broader view to understand their implications for the community. Planners do not seek to stem the technological tide; they work to ensure the most positive outcomes. Therefore, they need to be the center of collaboration, understanding whom to work with to accomplish their goals. Envisioning a positive, sustainable future is a fruitless activity unless an organization recognizes with whom it must collaborate to achieve that goal. Association executives must ask themselves: For this to be true, what also must be true? Who do we need to engage to create this outcome?

3. Become a master consensus-builder. Seeking public input while remaining objective is a core strength of planners. Good planning is inclusive, even of challenging people. Successful planners recognize that their primary asset is the public trust and engage in a consensus-building process based on shared goals.

   Association executives must foster a culture that encourages collaboration. Successful executives have a process or set of rules that facilitate consensus building. This often includes gathering supporting data from reliable, reputable sources, seeking a wide base of input, and ensuring that dissenting voices are heard. Consensus doesn't mean that a decision or course of action is the best for every individual, but rather it is the best for the community.

4. Consider technology to be just another acquired expertise. An interesting facet of the planning profession, Drinan says, is that planning is a multi-disciplined field. Planners need to understand geography, history, political science, law, engineering, communications, etc. Planners don't need to be experts in each of these fields, but they must understand how related issues impact the work they do. It is easy for association executives to be overwhelmed by technology, especially since applications are constantly being introduced. However, taking the time to learn about new products and how they impact the environment in which the organization operates helps to make the process more manageable. Technology vendors can be partners in this endeavor by providing education and hands-on demonstrations to association executives. Engaging vendors as partners in envisioning the future will lead to the biggest payout.

Food for Thought

- Has your organization identified the groups with which you will need to collaborate to realize future goals?
- Is your organization adept at building consensus?
- If not, what is holding you back? What could you, your staff and volunteers do to learn to be better negotiators?
- Does your organization strive to think broadly about the environment in which you operate and to study the business and economic issues that are impacting your members?

CHAPTER 5: BUILDING STRONG GOVERNANCE ONE STEP AT A TIME

Featuring: Abe Eshkenazi, CSCP, CPA, CAE, CEO, American Production and Inventory Control Society

Overview

The "supply chain" is a simple term that describes a complicated process. It refers to the journey a product makes from its origin as a raw material, such as steel or cotton, on through production to a destination that might be your local big box store or car dealership. Members of the American Production and Inventory Control Society (APICS) are the logistical wizards who plot that course. Supply chain professionals design, plan, execute, control, and monitor activities related to the delivery of products and services from creation to consumption.

APICS is a business association advancing both supply chain professionals and the companies they serve. Founded in 1958, the organization has steadily expanded its reach. Today it offers education, certification, information and networking benefits to professionals across the spectrum of supply chain activities. In addition, APICS serves corporate supply chain organizations by providing standards for developing processes and measuring performance, analytics, and research.

Public awareness of supply chain has increased due in no small part to news coverage during the 2008 recession. Dire economic forecasts about diminishing inventory, outsourcing and the loss of manufacturing jobs in developed economies made headlines alongside reports about the impact of international trade agreements such as the North American Free Trade Agreement (NAFTA).

While the recession reinforced the importance of supply chain to the global economy, it was hard on employees in the sector as well as on APICS. The decline in demand for products resulted in significant unemployment in developed manufacturing economies, particularly in the West. As a result, APICS' top line revenue fell from $22.6 million in 2007 to $17.9 million in 2009. To survive the recession, APICS' staff and volunteer leaders had to do double duty, working in tandem to respond to the challenging business environment while keeping an eye on the future to ensure the relevancy and sustainability of the organization.

Fortunately, APICS was successful and the association rebounded in 2010. As the global economy began to recover, supply chain became a significant competitive differentiator. APICS expanded its product portfolio, corporate services and global channel partner network. Growth was both organic and acquired. The association merged with three other research and industry organizations in the space of four years. Today, APICS is the largest global supply chain industry association.

APICS by the Numbers:

- $28.5 million annual revenue in 2016
- 45,000+ professional members in 100 countries
- 125,000+ certified professionals
- 190 chapters in North America
- 100+ international channel partners in 46 countries
- 2,000 active volunteers and partner leaders
- 100+ staff

The Road to Good Governance

When APICS CEO Abe Eshkenazi joined the organization in 2006, he was faced with a difficult situation. APICS was not running with the same precision that its members bring to their businesses. There was a disconnect between the board of directors and staff. A lack of trust had eroded communication to the point that even financial decisions were being negatively impacted. Eshkenazi spent his first six months with the organization interviewing former board members to get a better idea about what was causing the problems. "I knew that if I didn't fix the relationship issues, there was no future," he says.

It was clear that both sides had responsibility for the crisis in which the organization found itself. Still, Eshkenazi determined that his first and most-difficult-to-achieve priority had to be strengthening APICS governance. "I knew I could deal with the staff situation, but unless the board was aligned, it wouldn't make a difference."

Governance had always been a contentious issue for APICS. As far back as 2001, the board determined that its structure was working against it and attempted to address the problem. As a manufacturing-based association, APICS had taken a page from its own playbook by adopting a channel distribution model for its products and services. Certifications and education courseware were developed by the corporate entity but were sold and distributed at the local level through independent chapters. Chapters were divided into 14 regions across the United States, Canada and Mexico. Each region had a team of leaders who functioned as "staff," facilitating communication to the chapters. The APICS board of directors, at the time, had 22 members including the leader of each region plus officers and committee chairs.

Although the board knew it needed to change, determining how to implement improvements was difficult. A task force was assigned to make a recommendation. However, the task force, believing that form must follow function, suggested that the board develop a strategic plan prior to revising its governance structure. Based on the strategic plan that was drafted, the governance task force recommended that regional representation be eliminated in favor of board members who could provide specific expertise.

Change from within proved to be too difficult, and in 2003 the board rejected the recommendations of the task force. The situation continued to decline, with the executive director leaving the organization in 2005. Several vice presidents served as interim executives while board leaders became more active in trying to direct APICS' operations. As the board became more involved in the management of the corporate office, the staff became less engaged and less committed to the leadership's pet projects and decisions.

When Eshkenazi began his tenure as executive director, he was well versed in this troubled history. He came to the job understanding that governance was in dire need of an overhaul. More importantly, it was essential that the board accept that leadership was a primary responsibility and view it as a journey, not a destination.

Eshkenazi realized that no change could occur without first establishing a culture of trust and accountability. "If you ask staff, they will tell you at APICS we have one rule: no surprises. I will never wittingly surprise my board." Understanding that the entire organization needed to model that behavior, Eshkenazi asked staff to follow the same rule with him and with the committee leaders they support.

Confidence in Eshkenazi's guidance was also established by quickly addressing several of the board's priorities. A move from Alexandria, Virginia to Chicago provided an opportunity to do some needed staff restructuring. Other improvements included establishing key performance indicators and regular reporting systems for critical operations, such as product development and customer service. An ongoing strategic and operational planning process aligned with budgeting and staff goals was put in place.

In 2007, one year after Eshkenazi became CEO, the most controversial and complex change took place. With the goal of making the association's governance more effective and efficient, the organization's 14 regions were restructured into 9 districts. This move reduced the number of geographically based representatives to the board paving the way for additional changes.

The new directions improved the board's ability to govern, brought better communication with the staff and prepared the organization to respond aggressively to the 2008 recession. Although it wasn't easy, the board, committees and staff worked together to ensure that APICS not only survived the recession, but quickly rebounded and grew after the economy began to improve.

Ten years, three mergers and five significant changes to governance later, APICS is well positioned to take on the challenges of an environment in which the speed of change is unprecedented and emerging technologies are transforming how both supply chain and association professionals do and define their work. Governance at APICS has advanced not only due to changes in the board structure, but also because of the addition of board members from organizations with which APICS has merged. This smaller, competency-based board is focused on issues of strategic importance and supported by strong committees and an excellent staff.

Eshkenazi believes there is still more work to be done to position APICS to succeed in an increasingly competitive, global environment. Cultivating an entrepreneurial orientation is critical in an arena in which digital technology is giving many other players opportunities to engage the same audiences as APICS.

If Eshkenazi has a criticism of association management, it is related to the inherent bias toward the familiar, whether this traditional approach manifests in the nomination process or the development and delivery of products and services. Staff and volunteer leaders who bring an outside perspective to the work of the association create new possibilities. Without pulling any punches, Eshkenazi states, "Even though we know the benefits of creating diversity, it continues to be a major challenge for most associations. We gravitate toward like-minded individuals of similar backgrounds who share our experiences whether we are selecting new board members or hiring new staff."

While Eshkenazi is fond of saying that "nonprofit" is just a tax status and that associations should be run as margin-creating businesses, there is a reason he has decided to dedicate his work to advancing associations and, in particular, APICS. "I want to change the world and I believe that supply chain can change the world," Eshkenazi says. "I believe that what we do as volunteer leaders and as staff is important. It is so important that how we do it matters."

What Association Executives Can Learn From APICS

1. Governance is a journey that never ends. The APICS board knew that it needed to change long before Eshkenazi became the CEO. However, the change seemed too monumental. By meeting the board where they were and taking them where they needed to go, step-by-step, Eshkenazi has been able to gain their trust, improve their performance, and raise the level of discourse. As the supply chain environment changes, the board is confident it will be able to attract members who can lead the way. When taking a journey, it is helpful to take some time to chart a course. Association executives working with leaders on governance plans should be able to articulate both the starting point and the point of arrival. In addition, it's critical to understand that governance change often occurs in stages rather than major leaps. Leaders must understand environmental factors they will encounter along the way and establish a compass that helps everyone to know they are on the right path and understand how to adjust to unexpected issues and challenges.

2. Leverage your chair as a champion of change. Board chairs play an important role in motivating their colleagues to "be the change." Eshkenazi is the first to point out that he benefitted from a series of strong chairs who believed in the new governance direction and led by example. Executives can help board chairs fulfill this role by ensuring they are well prepared for board meetings, can keep conversations focused at the right level, and understand the contributions that they and other board members are making to the future of the organization.

3. Expect bumps along the road. Moving from a board whose members are elected by constituents in geographical regions to a board in which members are nominated by committee and approved by the board can be a bumpy road. At APICS, there were legs to this journey. Regions were consolidated into districts, then members-at-large were added. Eventually all members were at-large, responsible only to the best interests of the organization as a whole. In the transition process, the association was able to come to consensus on key decisions in which chapter interests differed from those of the corporate entity; chief among these was opening access to online education. It is important to understand that short-term losses may have to be endured to create a more sustainable organization in the long term. Accept the losses and move on.

4. Build trust on transparency. There is nothing that erodes trust faster than secrets or unwelcomed surprises. Therefore, Eshkenazi adopts a "no surprises" mentality with his boards. While Eshkenazi is clear that he has ultimate

responsibility for the operations of the association, he keeps the board fully informed of the decisions he is making and works with them to establish goals and objectives upon which they can evaluate performance. Many executives, especially at smaller organizations, struggle to keep their boards out of the association's operations. It either becomes a fight or they acquiesce. A first step is working with the board to agree about how much information they need to be comfortable with operation management. Mutually agreed upon executive performance objectives that are evaluated annually are also vital.

Food for Thought

- Does your association's board structure enhance or impede effective governance?
- Has your organization established a culture of trust? If not, what steps need to be taken to get on the right track?
- What are the strengths and weaknesses of your board's operations?
- What could you do to improve the effectiveness of your volunteer leaders?
- How could communication be improved between your board and your staff?

CHAPTER 6: MEETING THE CHALLENGE TO SYNCHRONIZE TECHNOLOGY WITH OPERATIONS

Featuring: Stephen Welch, Executive Vice President and CEO, American College of Chest Physicians

Overview

Murray Kornfeld had a dream that one day there would be an institution devoted to disseminating state-of-the-art research and education about diseases of the chest. After recuperating from tuberculosis, he dedicated much of his life to this purpose. Today the organization he founded in 1935, the American College of Chest Physicians (CHEST), more than realizes that vision.

The Glenview, Illinois-based association is a world-wide authority for both practitioners and patients on diseases of the chest. The organization provides information about pulmonary, critical care, and sleep medicine through its journal *CHEST*; year-round live and online courses; as well as books and mobile apps. Accredited by the Accreditation Council for Graduate Medical Education and the Society for Simulation in Healthcare, CHEST also is a center for simulation education. Its foundation supports clinical research and community service, patient education, and other philanthropic activities.

The CHEST community includes physicians specializing in pulmonary, critical care, and sleep medicine as well as broad-based representation of medical disciplines related to the chest. The organization's reach also expands to nurses, medical students, and many other industry professionals.

CHEST prides itself on an innovative approach that recognizes and responds rapidly to new demographics, evolving technology, and the shift from growing membership to growing engagement of the profession. Whether it's understanding the impact of Millennials on the market, meeting the demand to go mobile with education and communications, or expanding its customer base beyond the membership—CHEST's staff and volunteer leadership are creative problem-solvers who embrace growth and change.

CHEST by the Numbers:

- More than 19,000 members and 60,000 customers in 100+ countries
- CHEST Annual Meeting attracts 6,000 professionals
- The Innovation, Simulation and Training Center offers 6 labs, equipped with high-fidelity medical simulators, that mirror real ICU suites
- CHEST Foundation has raised $10 million for clinical research and community service since 1996

Synchronizing Technology and Operations

In four short years, CHEST gave itself a complete make-over—an accomplishment that might take another organization a decade. The first big venture was a move to a custom-built office in Glenview, Illinois. A new building and expanded space provided the opportunity for additional educational offerings and customization of member services. Updated learning management and content management systems were developed to deliver products more efficiently. In 2015, a new association/customer management system was launched to simplify the way the CHEST community engages online. As if that wasn't enough progress, CHEST also set out to globalize its content and clinical education. The accelerated timeline of these activities reflects the organization's belief in the value of synchronizing technology and operations.

CHEST's evolving customer model is central to these innovations. The organization's target audience has historically been private practitioners," says Stephen Welch, CHEST's executive vice president. "Now physicians are increasingly becoming employees of larger health care organizations. These organizations have point-of-care systems. So, we've needed to evolve our thinking about our customers to include these health care corporations. We need to serve these companies in order to serve health care professionals.

"It's more of a supply chain issue—it's essentially moving from a B-to-C model to a B-to-B model. The idea of thinking of the health care system as our customer directly impacts our content and services."

This shift does not mean that CHEST won't continue to offer long-standing membership options. According to Welch, "We can provide services and resources to people through different models; for example, we could offer an institutional subscription as well as the traditional membership model. What matters is reaching and engaging various audiences of caregivers, so they can use the information we have regardless of whether they're a member of CHEST."

Traditional membership has also evolved at CHEST. In the past, the CHEST community was physician-focused and structured on titles, degrees and clinical categories. Now CHEST welcomes all who provide clinical care for patients with chest disease. It's engaging physicians as well as other providers in the health care team.

Addressing Practice Trends

The rate of technological change is significantly impacting the way CHEST members practice. CHEST is continually updating its educational programs to reflect these advances. CHEST has been providing simulation-based, hands-on education for more than a decade. Its new state-of-the-art training center serves as a bridge from research and development to a realistic ICU experience. The center also offers hands-on skills training in procedures such as bronchoscopy and endobronchial ultrasound, a minimally invasive but highly effective diagnostic technique. In addition to CHEST-hosted programs, other societies can hold simulation training at CHEST. This allows the guest organization to construct the content and use their own faculty, without making the very costly infrastructure investment. Despite all the benefits, there are limitations to hands-on skills training—leading CHEST to consider other ways to optimize the experience.

"Hands-on simulation education is highly effective in small groups, such as 30 to 40 learners rotating through different stations, so they get a lot of one-on-one time with the faculty. This doesn't scale easily because you need a lot of faculty,"

Welch says. "So, we're trying to figure out how we can get more people to take advantage of training."

One strategy is to make CHEST's on-demand, online education more readily available so that learners don't have to attend a live session to access important information. CHEST is also aggressively studying how to deliver high-quality clinical education experiences to a wider audience. In the process, they are evaluating new partnerships with health care institutions to deliver simulations on a global scale.

Since CHEST is investigating moving from an audience of physicians to an audience of health care systems teams, they are seeking to identify the education requirements for these new groups. Earning and maintaining medical education credits is still important but discovering new opportunities will challenge the association to understand the next stage of virtual learning.

With the accelerated pace of technological change, big data is more important than ever for CHEST and for its constituents. "We launched a data analytics project a year ago, and created a data warehouse," Welch says. "We are looking to work with health care institutions and systems to provide ethnographic information and data on population studies, in addition to exploring other opportunities."

Culture of Change

Leadership and governance at CHEST have evolved over time to enable fast adoption and implementation of new technologies and ideas. When Welch joined CHEST 22 years ago, its CEO embraced innovation and entrepreneurial thinking. Subsequent CEOs have also been forward-thinking leaders, and the organization has continued to implement innovative systems and programs.

In 2009, a CEO change coincided with a major technology overhaul. The organization wanted to introduce learning and content management systems and to replace outdated association management software. A move to a cloud-based financial system was also on the docket.

"Information technology [staff] then reported to me and they spearheaded these IT platform projects," says Welch. "Because I was actively engaged in technology work through our publishing function, the IT team and I were tasked with determining how best to apply technology to all our organization's different functional areas. Now I am the interim CEO, and technology is at the forefront of everything we're trying to accomplish."

Publications have been a driving force in the association's decision making. When CHEST set out to globalize its content, research revealed that its customers didn't know who the American College of Chest Physicians was, but they were familiar with the journal. Welch says, "The journal *CHEST* was recognized then—and is still known today—for its clinical expertise, and we used that recognition to help rebrand the organization and increase the association's recognition among our constituents."

The way education is delivered continues to evolve. "We have changed our content and marketing strategy so that the right content is available to [constituents] at the right time on the right device. It was important to extend the philosophy of easy access to content beyond our publications," Welch adds. "We needed to think about how our constituents use information to provide care. For instance, they no longer enter data in charts—they are using electronic health records."

Overall, CHEST's governing board has been supportive and responsive to change. Some individuals have been risk-resistant, but the majority of the board historically has been willing to consider new ventures. "I think this is because when our constituents encounter changes within their profession, they can relate to the need for their association to also change," Welch says. "We also serve and work with clinicians who perform direct patient care, so they tend to have a lot of empathy."

That's not to say staff leaders don't need to make a convincing case to the board for changes. CHEST is a strategically focused organization with a plan that clearly identifies goals for improvements and innovations. "We always provide a business plan and a strong rationale for technology investments. We explain the investment and resource requirements as well as the benefits and reasoning behind why we are making the request—the [return on investment]. The board knows we aren't wanting to do something just because it's cool or it might make money, but because it's mission-based and will achieve strategic goals."

For example, the board supported CHEST's move from in-house technology systems to cloud-based platforms because the staff made a thoughtful business argument for this upgrade. Physicians, who were all moving to electronic health records, could also appreciate the benefits. Similarly, the board supported building CHEST's new headquarters and Innovation, Simulation and Training Center because they understood the importance of offering this state-of-the-art education. Welch notes that a track record of success contributes to the board's willingness to consider these requests.

Shaping Their Future

How does CHEST anticipate the future of work for its members? And how is it preparing them to navigate these changes?

"It's by making sure we are staying relevant and trying to anticipate the right thing," Welch says. "There are always competing priorities, new ideas and opportunities vying for our attention. So, we must determine what's really being implemented versus what's just a pipe dream."

CHEST takes periodic pulse checks by convening work groups to identify trends and constituent needs. The organization adjusts its education offerings based on this feedback. The goal is to always be on pace with advances in the profession. While CHEST must embrace new developments, it must also objectively evaluate whether techniques or therapies could pose a professional threat, without sounding an unnecessary alarm. "We considered having a medical futurist address our physicians at our annual meeting and talk about AI [artificial intelligence] technology. But after seeing some of those presentations, we reconsidered," Welch says. "I'm a little hesitant to bring the message to our physicians that, 'Hey, in the next 10 years you're all going to be replaced by IBM's Watson.'

"It's fascinating and a little scary that AI is going to do what a lot of our physicians do—read vitals, provide recommendations of when and how to administer certain care, converse with patients. At the same time, we can't put our heads in the sand and pretend it's not happening. It is happening—from AI interactions to telemedicine consultations. We just need to always ask 'How is this going to impact us as a profession?'"

What Association Executives Can Learn From CHEST

1. Technology works only when part of a larger strategy. Technology goals must align with other organizational goals. Strategic plans need to clearly describe goals for improvements and innovations against which potential technology investments can be evaluated.

2. Leaders can emerge from all backgrounds. Leadership needs may vary depending on the trends and environment in which constituents are operating. Organizations should cultivate individuals with unique backgrounds, perspectives and core expertise.

3. Broad staff leadership, buy-in, and involvement is essential for change to occur. Involving a broad cross-section of staff leaders and their departments in key decisions (e.g., choosing optimal technology solutions for internal and external use) will achieve buy-in and ensure that once the technology platforms are in place, they will function as intended.

4. A risk-taking culture is a must. The associations that are successful going forward must be committed to creating their own vision of the future. That means taking risks, taking control, and making decisions.

Food for Thought

- Is technology integrated into your organization's strategic plan?
- Does your organization's membership model need to change to accommodate your members' new business configurations?
- Are there new types of customers that your organization should embrace?
- Are your association's content and marketing strategies aligned with your members' needs?

CHAPTER 7: STRENGTHENING THE INNOVATION ECONOMY

Featuring: Gary Shapiro, President and CEO, Consumer Technology Association

Overview

What is the future of work? Ten years from now, will your job still exist? Will your industry be changed beyond recognition? These are big questions that .orgCommunity is exploring through its Association 4.0 research. While no crystal ball or soothsayer can make these predictions with absolute certainty, the Consumer Technology Association (CTA)™ is positioned to offer credible answers. The organization's ability to see beyond the horizon results from the nature of the profession it represents and its CEO leader.

CTA by the Numbers

- Membership includes over 2,200 companies
- 80 percent of members are small businesses and start-ups
- Other members are among the world's best-known brands
- CTA's annual CES® tradeshow has grown from 800,000 net square feet of exhibit space, 1,500 exhibitors, and 74,000 attendees in 1991 to 2.6 million net square feet of exhibit space, 3,800 exhibitors, and 180,000 attendees in 2017.
- Technology is a $292 billion industry supporting more than 15 million jobs in the United States.

The consumer technology sector, if not at the heart of growth in the United States economy, is a key factor in keeping it beating. There is no better proof that the economy and jobs loom large on Americans' minds, than the outcome of the 2016 presidential election. "Perhaps the biggest takeaway for me from the [President] Trump election is that a major part of our country felt overlooked," says CTA President and CEO Gary Shapiro. "We must remember technology's place in this."

In the past, the sentiment was that advancements in technology create new jobs to replace those that become obsolete. Shapiro believes that tit-for-tat scenario may no longer hold true. Self-driving cars provide one example of how the picture may have changed. Once the demand for autonomous vehicles takes off, driverless technology can impact the workforces of many different sectors. The breadth of enterprises that may be impacted by upending the auto industry include public transportation, the delivery and shipping of goods, vehicle manufacturing, body shops, highway patrol and other traffic law enforcement.

Technology and innovative online platforms may be threatened by overreaching mandates and outdated governmental regulations that result from industry's fear of potential job displacement. To address this issue, CTA produced the "New American Jobs Summit" in May 2017 in Washington, D.C. The event gathered policymakers, industry leaders, and key influencers to examine the future of employment in the United States. It explored how government and the private sector can collaborate to develop a competitive workforce, create new high-wage jobs and foster economic growth in the face of rapid technological innovation, an aging population, and increased global competition.

Shapiro notes that it's important for CTA to "educate policymakers to ensure the innovation economy is protected from laws and regulations which delay, restrict or ban the development of technologies." Currently, CTA is working with the federal government to preempt local and state laws restricting the operation of drones. Drones are used for a wide range of purposes, from agriculture to bridge building to delivering products, and much more. He also wants to prevent a patchwork of state laws governing the self-driving car.

Shapiro acknowledges that the tech industry and the leaders in government must be allies. In December 2016, tech leaders representing 1.3 million U.S. jobs and a total market cap of $2.9 trillion met with then President-Elect Trump to share interests and views on the biggest issues important to the country's economic success. According to a December 14, 2016, CTA news release: "The tech executives meeting with Trump are living the American Dream. Each of them achieved success through intellect, perseverance, and bold thinking...Trump values and respects the American Dream and its adjuncts: hard work, creativity, and entrepreneurship...Trump has a diverse business background and would likely restrict the runaway federal bureaucracy, which also frustrates many tech company CEOs."

Even so, Shapiro notes that since the election, he has witnessed the "greatest variation of optimism and pessimism that I've seen in a long time. No one wants to be negatively tweeted about" or criticized on social media platforms that have a large reach or are monitored by key customers.

"Large companies must be very careful of what they say, what they agree or disagree with—from immigration to LGBT issues. It is complex to navigate," Shapiro says. "There is some optimism, however. The stock market has done well since the election."

Reinventing Itself

As the association representing organizations that push the limits of traditional business models and create sea changes in legacy industries, CTA must continually reinvent itself. It recently embarked on two significant initiatives: overhauling its brand—including the association's name—and creating a council on disruptive innovation.

In November 2015, the association formerly known as the Consumer Electronics Association (CEA)® announced its new name—the Consumer Technology Association (CTA)™—and logo. Over the years, CTA has broadened its membership to include new technologies and intersecting industry segments, such as app and software development, crowdsourcing, content creation, personalized health care, the sharing economy, and music streaming services. By replacing the term "electronics"—which no longer captured the breadth of the consumer industry— with "technology," the new name more accurately represents its members, which include non-hardware innovators, such as BMW, Expedia, Ford, Google, Lyft, Netflix, Pandora, Snapchat, Starz, Uber, WebMD, Yelp and Twentieth Century Fox.

CTA has a history of evolving its name to reflect the changing dynamics of the industry it represents. The association began as the Radio Manufacturers Association in 1924, later became the Electronic Industries Association, then the Consumer Electronics Manufacturers Association and, in 1999, the Consumer Electronics Association.

Simultaneously with its most recent name change, CTA launched its Disruptive Innovation Council. The group is open only to CTA members that "exhibit a proven success, significant cultural impact and create new markets, solve or simplify commonly used processes or services." The Disruptive Innovation Council roster includes Boingo, Expedia, Inc., Google and a host of other companies that ride the cutting edge of invention. The council exists to communicate with and educate lawmakers, regulators and the public about the benefits that groundbreaking innovators bring to the marketplace. It aims to ensure that the best technology and ideas will not be delayed, restricted or slowed by "incumbent businesses using government to stifle progress."

"The pace of technological change is exponential and algorithmic," Shapiro says. "Smartphones are ubiquitous, and with the Internet, wireless technology and analytics [available at one's fingertips], anyone with tech skills and a broadband connection can create a new company." He points to Snapchat parent company Snap Inc.'s recent successful initial public offering and highlights Uber and Airbnb as examples of other breakthrough ideas successfully executed using existing technology.

"These companies are upending businesses. Other traditional businesses are reshaping their models and introducing new value propositions. Auto companies are one good example of businesses that have anticipated the future and radically changed their models."

The Council has developed a series of policy principles that will guide lawmakers and regulators in supporting a growing disruptive industry:

- Innovation should not require government permission.
- Intellectual property laws must balance protecting and incentivizing creators to innovate.
- Consumer privacy expectations and customized delivery can be achieved with clear disclosure, choice, and consent.
- Consumers should have the right to share opinions on services and products without concern for or fear of retaliation.
- Laws should enable innovation, not require perfection.

Enablers of Success

Shapiro has led the organization during the highest and lowest of economic times—from the tech boom to the dot-com bomb. When Shapiro became head of CTA in 1991, the organization had only 200 member companies, consisting mainly of TV set makers. "It was an old boys' club. I wanted us to expand in all ways." Now it has 2,200 members ranging from companies that manufacture drones, 3D printers, and self-driving cars to those producing wireless health capabilities and content creation.

The composition of its board also has changed. "It's as diverse as you can get," Shapiro says. "There are 10 different categories that we want represented on our board. Two categories relate to diversity. One category is diversity in the traditional sense, such as age, gender, race, and geographic location. The second is the business category, which includes company size, traditional industries, and new areas."

CTA's board members operate as enablers of success. They put aside personal and company interests to represent the group. That is a culture not easily replicated.

"The board must focus on the good of the industry. They must focus on big-picture questions. They must put away their company's interest and, at times, major public policy differences. This is our culture. It's industry and organization first over individual needs," Shapiro says. "My success has come because we have a board that is very focused on the future and, frankly, that may sometimes mean board members making decisions that create competition for their companies. Our board members are willing to swallow hard and stick with us."

Shapiro believes that CTA is one of a few exceptions in the association industry in its vision and ability to lead. "The association model is almost fully broken. That's because it's composed of thinking that's very, very old school. The typical board structure is focused on ego, micromanaging and day-to-day tasks instead of setting clear, objective standards, thinking strategically and empowering the CEO," Shapiro says. "Our board does not operate like a typical association board. We treat the board as incredibly important trusted advisors. I seek input when needed. We operate like a start-up company board. We welcome change. We thrive on change."

Shapiro recognizes that the board's expectation that he will freely give his opinion is unique in the association world. "I know other association CEOs who are not empowered, such as those representing the oil and petroleum and manufacturing industries," he adds. "They aren't empowered to answer questions or give opinions. They can't even issue a news release without the approval of volunteers."

There are two ways boards can work with their chief executive officers, Shapiro says. "Boards can allow the chief staff officers to do anything they want, or they can allow executives to do only what the board says they can do."

It comes down to trust, confidence, and success as well as risk-taking ability. According to Shapiro, "If you know where your industry should go, take a position, take a risk. I've never been in fear of losing my job. I'm passionate about the future of the country and the industry I represent. The longer someone is in the job, the more confident they get, and their board gets."

How does a new CEO establish the ground rules up front with his or her board chair and board? "The relationship that CEOs have with their boards is critical," Shapiro says. "I have a chart that I share at each annual board orientation. It explains what I do, what the board chairman does and what the board does. The board chairman doesn't have the authority to tell me what to do. The board chairman should not be telling employees what to do—their job is to get consensus to move the organization forward and take action. Boards have to be run right."

The search firm process is supposed to help determine cultural fit between the CEO and the board, Shapiro says. CEO candidates should ask the search firm how the CEO would be measured, how the board defines success, who determines where and when the CEO travels, as well as other process questions. "Then you get a sense of the organization," Shapiro says. "That understanding is really important for both sides."

In terms of operations, CTA also is an association anomaly. "We don't have a strategic plan. We have a one-page document of where we want to be in five years based upon what members we want and where we want to grow. We examine it two or three times a year as a reminder and often tweak it," Shapiro says.

"We set one-year operating goals in December, review them in March and often change things because the world has changed, and these goals become stale, stagnant and not valid anymore. We already tossed out two goals this year because they no longer make sense."

CTA also is a leader in workplace culture, largely due to offering nontraditional benefits. The association recently was named one of the 2017 *Best Places to Work in Virginia* by *Virginia Business* and Best Companies Group. This is the seventh consecutive year CTA has been honored by the program, which recognizes the 100 best places of employment in Virginia benefiting the state's economy, its workforce and businesses. CTA provides:

- Instructor-led boot camp, strength training and yoga classes as well as access to a 24/7 onsite gym at no cost to CTA employees
- A mortgage assistance program offering $25,000 toward a down payment of a primary residence within a five-mile radius of CTA's headquarters
- A tuition assistance program.
- Flexible summer hours
- A flexible work arrangement, including the opportunity to telecommute
- Generous matches for staff 401k plans
- Broadband reimbursement

Shapiro notes that even though the association is about consumer technology, the technology industry is still people-focused. "It's humans making decisions about who they hire, train, promote and award. We are committed to keeping our staff happy, healthy and motivated," Shapiro says. "This commitment helps us attract and retain the best and brightest as we continue our mission to grow the consumer technology industry and promote innovation."

What Association Executives Can Learn From CTA

1. Think like a start-up. Evolve as your industry evolves. Better yet, set the example of being agile, innovative and forward-thinking—don't wait to respond to change. Be the disruption.

2. CEOs: Run your board right. Set clear expectations and roles from the outset. Establishing trust takes time but providing the right framework to lead staff and deliver on strategic objectives will ensure fruitful and positive volunteer/staff leadership relationships.

3. Boards: Empower your staff leaders. Enable your CEO to lead by allowing full power to make all operating decisions.

Food for Thought

- Is your association keeping pace with the industry it represents? Are you ahead of or behind the curve?
- Is your relationship with the board effective? Are there conditions or issues that are impeding your ability to excel as a leader or to manage your staff?
- Is your organization's strategic plan serving its needs? Could your association benefit from replacing its strategic plan with some other type of planning process?

CHAPTER 8: MOVING BEYOND MEMBERSHIP

Featuring: H. Stephen Lieber, CAE, Former President and CEO,
Healthcare Information and Management Systems Society

Overview

From traditional roots, the Health Information and Management Systems Society (HIMSS) has become a hybrid that today is one of the nonprofit industry's most forward-looking organizations. Founded in 1961 as the Hospital Management Systems Society, the organization's diversified structure and truly impressive growth in engaged audiences and top-line revenue is guided by board and staff leadership that embraces innovative thinking.

HIMSS Divisions and Related Organizations

What makes HIMSS different from most associations is its multifaceted composition. The organization includes several divisions and wholly owned companies that provide a variety of products to related audiences. Notable among these are:

- HIMSS North America. Provides traditional association services including: professional development, networking, and leadership development and advocacy to constituents in the United States and Canada.
- HIMSS International. A division offering similar services to HIMSS North America for audiences outside of North America.
- The HIMSS Foundation. A philanthropy supporting activities in the areas of education, research and student engagement.

- HIMSS Analytics. A limited liability corporation (LLC) providing advisory services, including health care IT market intelligence, insights, and benchmarks.
- HIMSS Media. A business to business health care and technology media LLC that houses several brands, produces live events and provides information and analysis for senior health care professionals.
- Personal Connected Health Alliance. A separate 501(c)(6) association that develops technical standards for use by personal health and wellness devices.

HIMSS by the Numbers:

- Network of more than 1 million professionals
- 65,000 individual members
- 650 corporate members
- 250 not-for-profit affiliate member organizations
- 5 business units plus corporate (internal operations) services
- 10 office locations in North America, Europe and Asia
- 55 chapters across the United States, Puerto Rico, Canada and India
- 200+ new resources published annually

Expanding the Definition of Customer

A monumental part of HIMSS CEO H. Stephen Lieber's legacy since joining the association in 2000 is shifting the organization's focus from serving members to reaching, influencing and serving as many people as possible. "This is one of the fundamental changes associations need to go through," Lieber says. "[Associations] need to move away from limiting terminology that causes people to work in an old model and old way of thinking."

HIMSS began reaching beyond "member" to "audience" in 2002 by offering resources and benefits not exclusive to dues-paying professionals. It was an evolutionary process more than an overall strategy at the time, according to Lieber. By 2004, the philosophy of a broadening audience was becoming officially accepted and adopted. At a board strategic planning retreat, HIMSS' volunteer leaders concluded that to remain relevant and successful, HIMSS must reach as many people as possible. To achieve better health care through technology, non-member CEOs, CFOs and other clinical and management professionals must understand the value that technology brings to the table.

Respecting various audiences and "monetizing them" doesn't need to be a conflict, according to Lieber. In fact, it is an imperative to driving organizational profit and, in turn, using the revenue to achieve mission-critical goals. For instance, HIMSS Media and HIMSS Analytics have been able to deliver non-dues revenue while advancing knowledge in the industry.

Semantics of Growth

As early as 1990, HIMSS was already on the path of expanding the sphere of influence for health care IT by engaging in industry partnerships. The core competency of forming alliances paved the way for HIMSS to begin consolidating with other health care technology industry organizations and creating limited liability corporations, under the HIMSS corporate structure, to serve specific audiences. These groups may be based in geography (HIMSS North America and HIMSS Europe) or seekers of specialized information that can be leveraged to competitive advantage (HIMSS Analytics and HIMSS Media). In either case, the organization's extraordinary growth reflects its success at attracting and recruiting new constituents. HIMSS' accomplishments can be measured in terms of both new customers and improved financials. Last year, HIMSS had a total reported revenue of more than $90 million.

HIMSS' staff have been on an incredible journey, putting more than 10 other organizations under their umbrella since 2001. The integration of a media company with a staff of more than 60 individuals proved particularly challenging, both due to the size of the acquired company and the changing environment in which it operates. HIMSS had to simultaneously integrate a company and redefine its fundamental value proposition.

Autonomy and Focus

Business units enjoy significant independence and autonomy. This philosophy originates with an enterprise governance structure consisting of seven separate boards, each with the expertise to govern a specialized portfolio of products and services. "We developed a set of criteria to underpin our governance structure, and competency of subject is a fundamental skill," Lieber says.

Each of the companies is encouraged to avoid compromise and think about the future. "Everything reflects the philosophy of an entrepreneurial organization," Lieber says. Each business unit's management and boards are held accountable to a distinct set of metrics, whether mission- or margin-driven. "The general music is the same, but the harmony is different from one business unit to another."

Transparency and collaboration among the leadership is essential. Every week HIMSS executive team members issue a report summarizing work accomplished within their business units. This communication facilitates multifunctional work and collaboration. Still, conflicts can—and do—arise, especially in sales functions. Lieber recognizes that corporate clients generally like to work with one sales representative, but it is not always practical or in the client's best interest. It is difficult for one person to have the expertise to handle many products that are intrinsically different. "I try to make each business unit be very clear on what it can and cannot do so we do not run into conflict," Lieber says. "Role and scope definition are important."

Risk-Tolerant and Entrepreneurial

The issues that keep most association leaders up at night are the challenges that inspire Lieber to get up every morning. "I embrace change. It's the word I've use most often since I first came here 17 years ago." Lieber has worked with leaders and staff to make the organization change-oriented, risk-tolerant and entrepreneurial, as well as grounded in purpose. "At the first day of orientation, I tell new staff, don't be surprised if things happen one way today and another way six months later."

A challenge all associations share—HIMSS included—is the current proliferation of information. Associations position themselves as "the" source, but today, so many sources exist—many of them trusted. The ease and low cost of acquiring information on a variety of subjects is a trend impacting all elements of society. Associations must meet or exceed expectations for rapid information delivery, constantly changing interests and evolving demands, Lieber says. Above all else, to thrive and excel in the future, "Associations must be willing to expand their influence and recognize opportunities for growth."

What Association Executives Can Learn From HIMSS

1. There is a world beyond members. As the health care technology field exploded due to advancements and new health care information privacy regulations, HIMSS took advantage of the opportunity to broaden its sphere of influence. The switch in focus from member to audience created a context for significant organic and acquired growth. Association executives should ask themselves, "Who else needs to know about our work and the work of anyone related to our mission? How do we engage them? How do we monetize that relationship?" In the digital age, building audience is much easier than it used to be. But, it all starts by looking beyond the member to all audiences the association can serve.

2. Be fearless taking on the challenges of growth. Growth can be messy and in many cases it is more opportunistic than planned. Much of HIMSS' success is based on staying in tune with changes in the political, regulatory and economic environment of health care across the globe and determining how to get audiences the information and services they need, when they need it, so they can respond. Faced with similar challenges, many organizations find it easier to articulate why they should not engage, rather than why they should.

3. A fully integrated organizational structure may not be the best path to growth. HIMSS has seven separate boards with very specific areas of expertise. Staff supporting different business units have distinct objectives based on metrics. Business units have a good deal of independence and autonomy as a result of their specialization. When pursuing a path to growth through merger, associations will have to make decisions about how to integrate the organizations. If one plus one equals more than two, it may be important that the new business unit not be hamstrung by having to conform to existing operations. This can create positive tension that allows the company to grow in numbers, as well as advance operations.

4. Embrace purpose, run the business. For Lieber, nonprofit organizations are businesses and should be run as such. This means staying on top of industry and technology trends, as well as cultivating business acumen in managing both nonprofit and for-profit organizations. What is the difference between managing a nonprofit and for-profit business? Beyond tax requirements and net profit use, the answer may be "very little." For-profit businesses have a purpose. They serve a customer. They create value. Nonprofit organizations are the same. The skills and perspectives that make executives successful in the for-

profit arena are also required to be successful in the nonprofit arena. Executives need to challenge themselves to stay on top of their game.

Food for Thought

- Has your organization explored how it could expand beyond serving members?
- If you were to increase your sphere of influence, how might you go about getting the attention of new audiences, and what could you learn from them?
- If your organization has multiple business lines, are they given the autonomy they need to succeed?
- Is your professional development keeping ahead of your industry? Are you evaluating your own performance as often as you should? Do you actively seek feedback to stay at the top of your game?

CHAPTER 9: HUMAN CAPITAL – THE NEXT FRONTIER

Featuring: M. Bernadette Patton, CAE, Former President and CEO, Human Resources Management Association of Chicago

Overview

If you want to learn about careers in the Windy City, the Human Resources Management Association of Chicago (HRMAC) would be a great first stop. This organization keeps a finger on the pulse of Chicago's workplace. Established in 1915, HRMAC is the oldest HR membership organization of its kind in the United States. The association includes more than 700 local member companies representing over 7,000 area HR professionals. Members include employees at every rung on the career ladder, from senior executives in the corporate and consulting sectors to early careerists who will become future business leaders. HRMAC educates members to better understand and apply HR practices that drive business. The organization also serves as an authority on workplace developments impacting the Chicago area business community.

HR, which began as an administrative function, has evolved to become an important strategic initiative. The profession has grown beyond tasks such as payroll processing and planning office events to encompass the full spectrum of employee activities. HR departments are responsible for initiatives that directly impact business performance such as developing policies and procedures; managing compensation, risk and change; organizing training and professional development and overseeing globalization and corporate culture.

"The profession has grown to a better understanding of our organizations' financial drivers, customers and value propositions so that we can take a holistic approach to what we do," says longtime former HRMAC CEO, M. Bernadette Patton, who ended her 18-year career at HRMAC in June 2017.

During her 30 years as an association professional, Patton has proved that she understands how to evolve a profession. When Patton took over HRMAC in 1999, working with the board, she quickly implemented a new strategic vision, governance enhancements and high-level programming that has resulted in an increasingly engaged membership. The total number of HR professionals from member companies has tripled, and the number of members who actively participate in HRMAC in some way each year has reached 81 percent. The association's volunteer workforce, meanwhile, has grown from fewer than 100 in the early 2000s to more than 200 in 2017.

While many associations fail to change or simply outlive their usefulness, HRMAC remains relevant and current on issues that matter most to its members. The key is human resourcefulness.

HRMAC by the Numbers:

- 200 active volunteers
- 102-year-old trade association
- 700 local member companies
- Represents 7,000 area HR employees
- 81 percent of members actively participate in HRMAC each year

Human Resourcefulness

Patton, who led the primary organization addressing Chicago area workforce development and management, has a unique perspective on the future of association employment.

"Organizational needs are changing so quickly today, so associations must have the ability and fluidity to change," Patton says. "Whether it's with people or technology, we have to figure out how to be nimble. HR impacts the ability of a company to expand and change."

In past industrial revolutions, there was a lot of focus on an organization's physical assets—manufacturing, equipment and machinery. However, information is the power in our evolving knowledge economy, and human resources play an increasingly important role in business performance.

"There's a change going on in business. Organizations are realizing that people are the only asset that doesn't depreciate," Patton says. "The differentiator now isn't only the fastest piece of equipment or technology. It's having the best talent."

These days, the biggest trend for HR professionals involves attracting and providing the most optimal environments for workers. Flexible work preferences, actionable and frequent performance feedback, communication systems for remote teams, and incorporating technology advances are among the strategies businesses are using to attract and retain premium talent.

"Contingent workforce is a huge trend, and technology is supporting this shift," Patton says. "People want flexibility and companies want experts. Companies are parceling projects, hiring specialists and chaining the projects together. More work is being done remotely and people are enjoying that flexibility."

Integrated technology platforms enable all functional areas to communicate, access data, and work remotely while still providing high quality customer service—responding to customer demands faster and offering the individualized experiences that members expect. This also leads to an increased need for staff who can help find the sweet spot between not accruing enough data and information overload so that data is impactful," Patton says.

Another aspect of technology in the workplace that all organizations continue to grapple with is managing social media engagement, as it can be both a help and a hindrance to businesses.

"Organizations are challenged with how to manage social media so it has a positive effect on the brand for customers and employees," Patton says. "Some organizations are managing their Glassdoor postings proactively, so that potential employees have a true sense of what the company culture is like. At the same time, organizations must be responsive to employee comments, showing empathy, compassion and taking action when appropriate."

A Destination, Not a Casualty

HRMAC continually adapts its products and services to the changing needs of HR professionals. A prime example of this approach is how HRMAC became a go-to resource during the economic downturn of 2007-2008, when most companies were forced to do more with less.

Tough decisions about downsizing and saving money had to be made, and employees had to find ways to do their jobs successfully with fewer resources. HR played a tremendous role in those decisions, Patton says, and HRMAC assisted many organizations through the recession.

Because HRMAC was prepared and proactive in addressing the recession, the organization actually saw a spike in membership, event registrations and volunteerism during those troubled times.

In the years leading up to the recession, HRMAC recognized the power of its community and created two new membership categories designed to keep it intact. The first, Transition membership, was initiated in 2001 and is designed for individual members who are between jobs. Dues are reduced, and other discounts are provided. The second, Sole Practitioner membership, was created in 2003 and is for self-employed members and consultants. Introducing both these categories in advance of a disruptive time period helped HRMAC weather the storm.

"Although we are a company membership organization, individuals make the decision to join and they are also behind our products and programs," Patton says. "Well before the start of the recession, we recognized that people—long-time members—were starting to exit their companies, and that we were at risk of losing their knowledge and their participation because they had no way to stay active in HRMAC. So, we worked really hard to eliminate the barriers to participation."

When the economy faltered, HRMAC became a destination, not a casualty. "Because we had already built a community, when the downturn happened, people looked to HRMAC to build their network and find new jobs," Patton says. "And as people landed in new organizations, they brought their new companies to us."

HRMAC's Ability to Lead

Patton has been willing to take risks, engage people, and lay out a more strategic mission and vision. Before Patton's time, the board had significant administrative responsibility for the organization, limiting their ability to be strategically focused. They handled the minutiae of everything from meeting planning to newsletter production. For more than 80 years, HRMAC was not only governed by its board, but also run by it. Under Patton's leadership, a governance shift took place that allowed HRMAC board members to transform from volunteer labor into volunteer leaders. The board broadened the constituent base and engaged volunteers more robustly, enabling leadership to shift to a big-picture focus.

Having a board that governs instead of manages allows HRMAC to continue attracting the high-caliber leaders it needs to be more strategic, attract members, appeal to sponsors and develop programming.

"When you're thinking about joining an organization, one of the things you do is look at who else is a member," Patton says. HRMAC is diligent about recruiting the region's thought leaders to serve on the board. It also works to attract top HR officers in regional organizations not just to join but to actively participate.

To further free the board from its administrative duties, HRMAC expanded staff from two—Patton plus an administrative coordinator—to five, adding membership and professional development positions.

HRMAC's strategic shift continued with new and improved programs. The HRMAC Leadership Series, a three-part spring education series, was re-launched with a new format. Once a succession of "general meetings" focused on narrow topics, it was transformed into a package of high-level networking breakfasts featuring executive speakers discussing hot-button industry issues.

Several years ago, HRMAC started a future leaders program, creating the next generation of outstanding HR executives. It focuses on bringing together and developing high-potential future chief HR officers across Chicagoland companies. About 20 percent of program participants have had internal career moves after their program participation.

In 2008, the association introduced two new awards: Volunteer of the Year Award and Leader of the Year Award. The volunteer award came out of the need to recognize and incentivize the 200-plus people who regularly invest their time and effort to further HRMAC's mission. The leader award honors a professional—a CEO or other executive, outside of HR—who has been a champion of HR in their company. "It was designed to create a dialogue with the broader business community and gives us a chance to elevate the conversation outside the HR arena to tell the story of human capital strategy and help other business leaders understand its value," Patton says.

Patton also made it her mission to create an organization that is a career destination. "We worked hard to recruit a high-caliber board of industry experts, which has motivated people to want to be involved with HRMAC," she says. The board reflects the community in sector, ownership structure, geography, and gender and ethnic diversity. In 2016, HRMAC created a millennial board member seat so that the perspective of this growing demographic is represented at the strategic level.

"HR diversity and inclusion are very important. HRMAC is a conscious leader in this area. We reflect the universe of our world," Patton says. "You have to model what you want your members to be. For us, this meant breaking the mold by putting a young leader on the board who is not an executive.

"For the most part, companies want to engage and understand the value of a diverse workforce—and that definition is expanding," Patton says. "Are associations as committed to diversity as their company members are? They should be. Companies have affinity groups that help support diversity. Associations must do the same thing, whether formal or not, so that people can see themselves represented in their association and want to belong."

What Association Executives Can Learn From HRMAC

1. Give HR a seat at the strategic table. HRMAC advises all their member companies to do this so that HR leaders have a clear understanding of the organization's financial drivers, customers and value proposition. Armed with this knowledge, HR professionals can make better recommendations regarding performance management, compensation planning, risk and change management, training and professional development, globalization and corporate culture—which all contribute to creating a nimble organization and driving higher business performance.

2. Recruit the best talent—people are your organization's differentiator. Everyone has technology, but not everyone has the right talent to serve its customers and achieve strategic goals. Even the best, most robust systems and the newest technology won't have the intended impact unless you have the right personalities with the right drive and experience behind the controls. The process of identifying the talent and the attributes of an ideal staff may vary from organization to organization, but HRMAC and its members believe the "people" fit is more important than the technology fit. Of course, processes and systems are also essential to an organization's success, but it's people who drive process, procedures, the use of technology and the harnessing of data to make course corrections or validate actions and strategies.

3. Consider a contingent workforce. People want flexibility, and companies want specialists. More companies are parceling projects, hiring specialists and chaining the projects together instead of having full-time positions with a broad range of responsibilities.

4. Transform your volunteer labor into volunteer leaders. Have the board relinquish its tactical responsibilities to committees and interest groups so it can govern instead of manage. Since the HRMAC board did this nearly 20 years ago, it's had a more thoughtful, measured guide for developing and assessing the impact of its programs, services and offerings.

5. Become a conscious leader in diversity and inclusion. That can mean reflecting the universe of the profession you serve or modeling what you want your profession to become. If people see themselves represented in their industry's

association, they will want to belong. For instance, HRMAC recently created a millennial board seat to ensure it is addressing the demographic's needs at the strategic level.

Food for Thought

- Is your association's membership structure designed to weather an economic disruption?
- Is your board focused on strategy and governance? If not, what is keeping them in the weeds?
- Does your leadership reflect your industry's population in terms of age, ethnic and gender diversity?
- Does HR have a seat on your management team and participate in planning and decision making?

CHAPTER 10: HEATING UP THE FUTURE

Featuring: Tom Morrison, CEO,
Metal Treating Institute

Overview

From your coffee maker to your computer and your car—you are surrounded by products produced by members of the Metal Treating Institute (MTI). Heat treated metal is used to create the machinery of modern life. Processed metal plays a role in the aerospace, agricultural industries, in addition to almost every other major industry.

MTI is a nonprofit trade association that represents the largest network of commercial heat treaters in the world, with plants in 40 states and eight countries. The organization is active in government advocacy and technical standards, conducts national and regional educational networking conferences, and produces the Furnaces North America business exposition every other year.

Since its inception in 1933, MTI's top job has changed hands only four times. The last transition took place in 2008. Tom Morrison replaced M. Lance Miller, J.D., CAE, who retired after 31 years as CEO. MTI had hired Morrison in 2005 to lead the organization into the future. Since then, membership has expanded worldwide and includes commercial heat treaters, manufacturers with in-house heat treatment operations and suppliers that provide products and services to the industry.

MTI is firmly focused on future technology and employment in the heat-treating sector. It strives to stay ahead of the tech curve in both heat-treating processes and in serving members of all generations.

Embrace Change, Respect Tradition

A core value at MTI is to embrace change and respect tradition. Those might seem like contradictory beliefs, but Tom Morrison leads by continually striking this balance as he works with the personalities on his board and staff to advance members' business interests.

In Morrison's discussions with association leaders across the country, he has learned that, "Personalities can get in the way of success—that's what holds back many associations from growing," Morrison says. "Sometimes when you're successful as the executive, the old guard begins to feel like you've become larger than the organization. They just don't see it as the leader being successful, caring for the group and moving it on to great things. They view it as the association becoming more about the CEO's success than the association thriving.

"Then [the board] starts to put on the brakes and handcuffs and pull you back, because in their mind the association has gone from the control of the volunteers serving it to the association executive. It all boils down to personality. When personality gets in the way of the purpose, it's the beginning of the end of the purpose."

Morrison's success with a diverse board is part good governance and part good business.

"The average executive director or CEO is too afraid to challenge their board. They are great at governance, but not business savvy," Morrison says. "I always ask people, 'How do you think the association would be run if Steve Jobs or Bill Gates was the CEO?' It would be run very differently. We, as association executives, need to be business savvy. We need to predict the next major shift and anticipate changes.

"That's what I've strived for, and that's why I consistently push our board. We've constantly got to be thinking what it is that our members are going to need five years down the road so that we can be ready. Our board is not slow to move. They understand how fast the future is coming at them. We live in the future and act today."

When it comes to strategic planning and prioritization, MTI filters everything through its "hexagon."

"Organizations should identify and focus on no more than six things they can do better than anybody else. Otherwise, their secret sauce gets watered down," Morrison says. "We just happen to have six pillars or things we do better together than anyone else in our space. Our members can't do these things without us. They realize through MTI they can achieve more and better results collectively than they can by themselves."

MTI's six strategic pillars are:

- Actively recruit, develop and engage younger members
- Stay ahead of the technology curve in heat treating processes and serving the members
- Promote contract heat treating to the captive market
- Educate and influence governed and other regulatory bodies
- Evaluate and promote services to MTI members
- Promote membership to prospective members and other allied groups

If an opportunity is presented that can potentially solve friction, anxiety or stress in members' business, MTI will look deeper into that endeavor to determine whether it fits into the strategic hexagon.

"We don't invest in potential, we invest in known solutions to help with our members' critical, known problems," Morrison says. "Most people are running around trying to fill perceived value. That is dangerous. You've got to find your actual value. When you find your value, what's meaningful to your members, then membership engagement and recruitment is not a big deal."

Trends Impacting MTI Members

Technology advancements, generational shifts, and the current political landscape are all impacting the business of MTI members. Morrison sees it as MTI's duty to spur conversations about anything that has a bearing on the heat metal industry.

In March 2017, MTI began a monthly live webcast, "Heat Treat Tuesday." The first two topics addressed were how additive manufacturing and 3D printing will change heat treating, and the impact of technical specification changes on quality.

"We've had speakers at our conference, shared YouTube videos and other intelligence to address disruptors like 3D printing as well as topics such as how to be a manufacturer of the future," Morrison says. "We're forcing the conversation." The impact of 3D printing is an unknown for many industries. Morrison believes the technology may create big opportunities for some industry organizations. "But if it can produce the perfect part without heat treating, then that is troubling to our community, and can create a lot of opposition and non-business," he adds.

Some members pride themselves on being at the leading edge of shop technology—automating and modernizing everything from their manufacturing processes to management software. One member shop in Phoenix boasts it is "digital in everything it does."

The transformation to digital formats is desirable "because members want all their information to be shareable, documentable and transferable at a moment's notice; they don't want to rely upon a piece of paper," Morrison says. "If a customer calls and says, 'Hey, you didn't ship us enough of a particular part,' the company can provide a picture and video showing what came out of the oven. Modernizing processes solves many customer service problems."

While MTI itself harnesses technological advancements to better connect and inform MTI members, it is also focused on future member expectations—and those of its current largest demographic, Generation X.

"Right now, 75 percent of the association makeup is Generation X. But all associations are fixated on the Millennials. However, the majority of Millennials are still in their 20s. How many of you joined anything in your 20s? We all joined things in our 30s, and the biggest mistake every association has made is not looking out for people who are now 33 to 53," Morrison cautions.

"Instead, associations are trying to sell membership to a group who isn't prepared or doesn't have the money to buy. They have skipped showing how awesome and valuable they are to Gen X. You can't build your entire structure based upon the Millennials who will be here in 5 or 10 years and forget that Gen X is the here, the now. They are the members that join today. They are the ones who are going to be on our board today. They are the members looking at us today and we're not addressing them."

That said, Morrison notes MTI members are looking forward to more Millennials entering their 30s and enjoying greater disposable income.

"If they are going to start spending that money, then we're going to have a record number of products being made in the United States," Morrison notes. "Our business owners are cautiously optimistic, however, because business has flatlined the last few years due to demographics. Gen X has 12 percent fewer members than Baby Boomers. So, we've had less prospects to choose from for about 10 years."

Morrison purposely uses the term "members" versus "customers" because he still believes in the membership model.

"Don't listen to people who say the membership model is dead. There's no other model that allows you to come together as a group of people or companies and facilitate or fight for a cause." Morrison believes that the associations that struggle with recruiting members are challenged because they haven't figured out how to sell the power of that group dynamic.

MTI members also have been cautiously optimistic about the new political landscape.

"We believe a certain amount of regulation and oversight is necessary for establishing baseline levels of safety, quality and fair ways of doing business, but we are encouraged that some unnecessary regulations will be removed under the new administration," Morrison says. He is also closely watching the economy and what is being done to spur growth. When people have more buying power, it stimulates manufacturing. "And that means more manufacturing with metal that needs to be heat treated, which translates to more work for our members."

What Association Executives Can Learn From MTI

1. Because times are changing rapidly, it is imperative that associations be run by business-savvy leaders. MTI constantly considers what members will need five years from now, so it can be ready to offer those services.

2. Identify three to six things your members can't do without you, and focus on just those things. When it comes to strategic planning and prioritization, MTI filters everything through its six strategic pillars. "Organizations should identify and focus on no more than six things they can do better than anybody else. Otherwise, their secret sauce gets watered down," Morrison says.

3. Focus on Gen X, not Millennials. "Right now, 75 percent of the association makeup is Generation X. The majority of Millennials are still in their 20s. They are not prepared to join [associations] or don't have the money to buy services," Morrison says. "[Associations] have skipped showing how awesome and valuable they are to Gen X. You can't build your entire structure based upon the Millennials who will be here in five or 10 years and forget that the Gen X is the here, the now. They are the members that join today."

Food for Thought

- How does your association strike the balance between tradition and change?
- Are you able to have candid discussions with your board about the need for change or other challenging topics?
- If not, what steps could you take to improve that dynamic?
- What has your association done to address the needs of Gen X? Of Millennials?

CHAPTER 11: WHERE QUALITY IS KING

Featuring: Stephanie Mercado, CAE, Executive Director and CEO, National Association for Healthcare Quality

Overview

Although members of the National Association for Healthcare Quality (NAHQ) work in vastly different settings, they have one thing in common. The status quo is never good enough. They are the people whose job is to ask: How can we work better, faster and smarter, and what can we do to improve outcomes and reduce costs?

Founded in 1976, NAHQ is the only organization dedicated to advancing health care quality. It is also the sole provider of an accredited certification in this discipline, the Certified Professional in Healthcare Quality® (CPHQ).

Health care quality professionals work in a variety of settings—from hospitals and clinics, to government agencies and academic institutions. They are involved with the strategic and administrative tasks affecting patient safety, risk management, policy compliance, performance measurement, process improvement, and information management. These responsibilities involve critical activities related to patient safety such as hospital-acquired–injury prevention, infection control practices, electronic medical record accuracy and individual health care provider performance.

Continuous quality improvement is a core value for both the members and their association. A quality mindset permeates all NAHQ's operations and offerings.

NAHQ by the Numbers:

- More than 7,000 members; 40% membership growth since 2011

- $5.8 million operating budget
- 22 full-time equivalent employees
- Chief revenue sources: certification (30%), membership (25%), education programming (21%)
- More than 10,000 CPHQs; 30% increase in CPHQs since 2011
- NAHQ's reach has grown significantly—from 11,000 in 2014 to more than 30,000 in May 2017.

A Quality Mindset

Both the health care and association management industries have entered a period of rapid evolution. NAHQ is riding this tide along with them by using innovative thinking to adjust to and navigate the rapid changes.

"We're experiencing the consolidation of health care delivery from a provider perspective, so much more alignment and connectivity is needed throughout the continuum," says Stephanie Mercado, NAHQ's CEO and executive director. "As a result, more health care quality professionals are needed to improve quality and lower costs across the system. Within historically vertical silos, this change is showing up as a shift to care coordination, predictive health care data analytics, and population health."

Consolidation of health care systems and new delivery models are creating a different paradigm for NAHQ members. "They're not working in vertical silos anymore. Instead, there is a melting pot of professionals all contributing to quality from across the care continuum. These individuals are seeking support to understand emerging roles and functions and to have access to tools that show how to perform effectively," Mercado says.

The health care quality profession took root 40 years ago, with its beginnings in chart abstraction and retrospective analysis. The shift toward a prospective orientation at a higher level of performance is changing the workforce in a major way.

Some individuals with traditional roles are eager to move in this direction, while others have been unable or unwilling to make the transition, Mercado says. A new demographic from traditional sources of health care, and interestingly, from other industries like manufacturing and operations, is being ushered in to fill the vacancies.

"Now what we have are individuals who know health care but not quality, and individuals who know quality but not health care," Mercado says. "The health care market needs one thing from these diverse individuals: a coordinated and competent workforce. So, the question we've been addressing is, "What are we going to do to support them?"

Supporting Members

NAHQ recently commissioned a market research study that indicates few members and customers have a clear understanding or definition of health care quality. "They don't know what their job function should be in this evolving environment, and often, neither do their supervisors. It's all they can do to adapt to the changing needs through education and training, let alone consider their own career trajectory," Mercado says.

That creates an opportunity for NAHQ to provide additional services. Since its founding, the organization has defined, taught, and certified health care quality. Now it must do this job in ways that resonate with the current marketplace and respond to the health care evolution. It's clear to Mercado that the focus on value— where quality meets cost—will continue to be paramount in any health care model. "We're trying to provide comfort to our members, letting them know the quality toolkit isn't changing," Mercado says. "What's changing is the way the toolkit will be deployed to solve typical and emerging challenges in health care."

Since the 1980s, NAHQ has helped health care quality workers prepare for and advance their work through the CPHQ certification. Certification indicates an individual's competence in health care quality at a mid-level. In the last two years, NAHQ has developed the concept of expanded competencies. The organization has begun to identify proficiencies and products for members at the entry and advanced skill levels. New offerings include a Healthcare Quality Principles Certificate Program for beginners as well as competency training and published resources in six advanced and master practitioner levels. As a group, these topics define the future of health care quality: data analytics, population health, performance and process improvement, regulatory and accreditation, and care transitions across the continuum.

"The competencies address not only where health care is at, but where it is going," Mercado says. "We want to help in a way that really meets today's need, which is to define, to teach, and to certify health care quality." One NAHQ volunteer who is responsible for seven health care sites is using NAHQ's "HQ Essentials: Competencies for the Healthcare Quality Profession" publication as a framework to build her staff structure, including developing job descriptions, evaluations, and performance reviews.

NAHQ also created profiles of health care quality professionals so people can understand the various jobs available, the real people who are performing them, and the qualifications and training that are involved.

Mercado also recognizes that NAHQ must address the increasing need for better data analysis and methods of using it for maximum impact. "There is an opportunity to teach and certify how health care quality professionals can use data and other intelligence to promote change and convince health care leadership to do things differently," she says.

Another challenge the industry will continue to address is the increased ability for systems to integrate and share information. "This is paramount because of the health care connectivity trend," Mercado says. "Right now, electronic medical record devices and other systems are not all connected, leading to a lot of redundant work and missed opportunity. You have software for claims data, for incident reporting, and for incident prevention. It's complicated, but health care quality professionals will help figure it out."

Refining the Market

In the health care quality market, we are finding that people are less "like-type" and more "like-minded," Mercado says, making it difficult to identify the NAHQ audience universe. Therefore, value proposition has become NAHQ's number one focus, creating programs and service around what Mercado calls, the "good-fit" members.

"No one graduates with a degree in health care quality. Very few master's degree programs are offered, although they are popping up more and more," Mercado says. "Because members self-select based on their interest in health care quality, we end up with good-fit members and bad-fit members. Figuring out the good-fits is important to us because as a $6 million organization with diverse member needs, we can't be all things to all people. We must be really tight on who we are, what we do, and who we do it for."

When Mercado joined NAHQ in 2013, its annual membership attrition was high, averaging 31 percent. It was recruiting only a few more members than it was losing every year. Mercado considered what would happen to NAHQ if it could retain those members who are prone to leave. "I wondered what that would look like and how fast we could grow if we retained at a higher rate," Mercado says. "That was the beginning of our intense focus on value proposition."

Mercado acknowledges that while it's tempting for associations to model their offerings after competing organizations, that approach is counterproductive. "NAHQ volunteers and members often send me information on training other groups are providing, suggesting NAHQ should do this too. I generally respond that the program is great for them, but that's not who we are," she says. "We define, we teach, we certify. If we focus on being [other organizations], then somebody else will be us. We just need to be us and do that well in a very disciplined way."

Because of health care system consolidations, new customers are emerging. NAHQ is exploring how to keep a relationship with members who need individual support and to expand its offerings to institutions. Many of the new organizational members are led by NAHQ members and CPHQs.

Nimble Governance

NAHQ needed to grow fast in an increasingly competitive environment. One of Mercado's objectives was to restructure the organization, so it would be able to quickly shed operations and services that no longer work, reinvest in successful offerings, and build on new opportunity. Part of the solution was changing the association's governance structure.

"We now use a matrix governance model so that the goals, objectives, and strategies are aligned to NAHQ's macro plans, and not individual committees. This way we don't have committee structures with subspecialty brutes and territorial issues that prevent the organization's mission from moving forward," Mercado says. Historically, NAHQ committee chairs served one-year terms and reported to the board. "Short terms and limited alignment at a level below the board caused NAHQ to lose traction frequently," Mercado says.

Now goals and objectives are not assigned to commissions—they are assigned to the organization. "If you align goals vertically in a functional area, the opportunity for leverage will be lost," Mercado says. "We're now doing a lot of cross-functional work. We're assigning a staff project manager and, as appropriate, a volunteer, to stay on track. We're focused on an outcome rather than a deliverable."

For instance, NAHQ has a goal of ensuring a competent, coordinated work force that is prepared to meet the needs of healthcare quality across the continuum. One of the objectives is to bring together different groups of professionals in quality roles. The strategy to deliver on this objective is to arm these different groups with the required skills and tools to perform work consistently and reliably. "Now we focus on two big goals and use everyone's support in executing them," Mercado says, "instead of trying to accomplish 50 different things that create a land grab for resources and prioritization, in which the person with the loudest voice wins. When we focus on the organization and measure what matters, politics are limited, and we can be nimble.

"And, through the matrix model, all NAHQ commissions feel like they're contributing. Everybody's engaged because everybody has a role in almost every activity and/or they can see how their effort leveraged the next step."

"Outside of our standing governance structure, project- or task-level volunteers are providing their services in a 'just-in-time' manner," Mercado says. "Volunteers don't have the time that they used to have. They love to collaborate and participate with other people by doing what they do well and offering their perspective in a very precise way," Mercado says. "Then they step aside and let the next person come in; support-level tasks are assigned based on need, not terms."

Varied member expectations and career mobility were other motivators in changing NAHQ's governance structure. "People are expecting different things from an association. Loyalist members are less prevalent," Mercado says. "People are looking for more of a subscription service to acquire resources and tools. Many don't want to belong in the traditional sense of growing up with peer groups, moving through association hierarchy, becoming the president of the organization. Today, people are dodging and weaving in their careers; that's causing them to move in and out of different associations, so we professionals must think differently about what membership means."

While NAHQ's eye is on the future, it also doesn't want to completely shed tradition.

"We are always trying to keep change in balance, and not lose the fabric of the association in terms of the roles of the staff, the association management, the board, and governance," Mercado says. "There's a lot that I think shouldn't change. But I also think that the way associations have traditionally operated has caused them to be slow and reactionary, and not the best stewards of our members' resources. I think we can do more if we approach the execution a bit differently."

What Association Executives Can Learn From NAHQ

1. Make value proposition your number one priority. Associations end up with good-fit members and bad-fit members. Figuring out the good-fits is important because most small- to mid-size associations can't be all things to all people. Become more focused on what you do and who you do it for.
2. Resist the temptation to model the competition. It ends up doing the association a disservice. If you focus on being like other organizations, another organization

will focus on being like you. Be "you" and do that well and in a very disciplined way.

3. Focus on only two to three large goals and use everyone's support in executing them. Don't try to accomplish 50 different goals that can create a land grab for resources and prioritization.

4. Provide "just-in-time" volunteering. Volunteers don't have the time that they used to have. Enable them to collaborate and participate by doing what they do well and offering their perspective in a very precise way.

Food for Thought

- What is your association's value proposition? Are you focusing sufficient attention to that area?
- Does your governance structure help or hinder your progress towards goals?
- What activities would make your association better prepared to respond quickly to changes in your members' needs and the business environment?
- Are you creating the best possible experience for volunteers?
- What could you do to enhance the volunteer experience?

CHAPTER 12: LIFE IN THE FAST LANE

Featuring: Gail Rutkowski, Executive Director,
National Shippers Strategic Transportation Council

Overview

Members of the shipping industry live in the fast lane in more ways than one. They are the people who manage transportation across the roads, rails, oceans, and skies. The need to consistently do that job better means that they must either adopt new technology or collide with it.

The National Shippers Strategic Transportation Council (NASSTRAC) is a 501(c)(6) trade association serving members who are responsible for moving their company's freight efficiently and cost-effectively through the supply chain. Retail, manufacturing, food and beverage, pharmaceutical, and chemical industries are among the many businesses it represents.

NASSTRAC "Regular" members are the primary organizations that the association serves. They include manufacturers, retailers, wholesalers, and distributors, as well as third-party logistics companies. Associate members represent ancillary businesses such as the providers of transportation, warehousing or technology services.

The last two decades have been among the most challenging for NASSTRAC since its founding in 1952. Rapid innovation, exploding technology, expanding globalization and shifting societal trends have revolutionized the way Americans use the nation's transportation system. Along with the benefits of these changes come increasing complexity and the need to assess, evaluate, and adopt new paradigms even before they are fully realized. These trends are ongoing and accelerating— making it imperative for NASSTRAC members to be both effective movers of products and agile thinkers who willingly confront disruption and change.

Driving Change

eBay, Amazon, Etsy and the myriad other online rule-breakers that turned the retail business on its head are also driving relentless change in the transportation industry. Customers are being conditioned to expect instant gratification. Yesterday's standard 5- to 7-business day delivery won't stand up to competition when everything from a perfectly prepped dinner ready to pop in the oven, to a suite of kitchen appliances is just a click away. More than 69 percent of Americans shop online each month for clothes, food, home goods, and more, according to Gail Rutkowski, executive director of NASSTRAC.

"Common sense solutions to increase shipping capacity are necessary as more consumers realize the benefits of e-commerce and America's existing transportation infrastructure struggles to keep up with the expanding needs and demands of a changing and growing nation," Rutkowski says.

On the private sector side, this means NASSTRAC member companies must continue to invest in new technologies, including upgraded fleets and more, to ensure the nation's transportation system is as efficient, reliable, sustainable and safe as possible. On the public sector side, it is NASSTRAC's hope that the current White House administration's emphasis on infrastructure will relieve stress on America's interstates and highways, reduce congestion, and enable companies to ship more goods per trip.

"We spend a lot of time on federal advocacy, conveying the voice of the shipper and collaborating with other organizations," Rutkowski says. "NASSTRAC collectively communicates shippers' concerns to public policymakers with greater impact and at a lower cost than if each shipper member acted alone."

A recent concern for shippers is the increasing fragility of the supply chain and its transportation providers in general. Extreme weather, political unrest and more mundane glitches such as shortages or productivity issues are just a few of the threats to smooth operations. While ocean carriers and ports have been the primary hubs of disruption, shippers also need to keep an eye on motor carriers, both local and long-haul trucking.

"The carriers that shippers use, and their financial stability can make a big difference. The time is coming when if a carrier isn't being compensated for surge or insurance capacity, they simply won't offer it," Rutkowski says. "What this means for shippers is that their transportation providers are much less resilient than they used to be."

Seventy percent of goods in this country move on a truck, so trucking is one of NASSTRAC's primary focus areas. The organization is working with lawmakers to develop a regulation to allow "pup" trailers to increase in length from 28 to 33 feet.

This would reduce the volume of vehicles on the road as well as the number of drivers.

"We have had a driver shortage for 10 to 15 years. The average age of truck drivers now is 55," Rutkowski says. "Despite pay increasing over the past three years and attempts to incentivize younger truckers, it remains difficult to attract commercial drivers."

The fastest growing segment within the industry right now is third-party logistics companies. "A lot of shipping professionals are moving from shippers to third-party logistics companies," Rutkowski says. "We are losing our base of knowledgeable shippers. Shippers need to be aware and learn about these issues."

The "Uberization of freight" also is a hot topic in the industry. Members wonder whether Uber will put on the gloves with the shipping industry as it has in the consumer marketplace, Rutkowski notes. "Uber has bought autonomous trucks, and they are already being tested. For instance, when transporting freight, there are three trucks: a driver-operated vehicle in the front and back, and an autonomous-driven truck in the middle. "Platooning," as this practice is known, could impact freight transportation in a big way. There are a lot more regulations to consider in terms of freight versus people."

Planning for Disruption

Supply chain disruptions are unpredictable. Financial distress, operational mistakes, natural disasters (an ever-growing threat due to climate change), or an unexpected uptick in demand are among the many issues, both large and small, that can derail a shipment. Rutkowski believes one of the key factors in managing the unexpected is to plan for it.

"Now, you can't divine every scenario, but you can identify the possibility of major disturbances and construct a response," Rutkowski says. "Having a sound business continuity plan helps. Creating tabletop enactments of those situations helps even more. The industry must focus on innovations that support the business goals of companies through smart transportation. In our industry, you're only as good as your last shipment."

Along with chills and thrills, the technological roller-coaster also brings some significant benefits. Sensors and GPS devices are dramatically improving the shipping industry. "You can track trucks anywhere in the country with GPS. Fleets can gather information such as how long trucks are idling, the number of hard stops they make, turn times, etc. It helps folks improve their decision making and get better at their jobs. It also points out clogs in companies' supply chain systems and indicates what's causing a company to lose time on deliveries."

Rutkowski sees tensions among older shippers accepting change and technology, yet it's been a challenge to attract younger people, who may be more comfortable with innovations, to join NASSTRAC.

"Our membership has been stagnant for the last few years. The challenge is on the company side," Rutkowski says. "Many companies won't pay hundreds or thousands of dollars for their employees to join or continue membership. They see association conferences as boondoggles. Leaders are afraid professionals will go to the conference, network, and find a new job. It is very difficult getting shippers engaged for several reasons; young people entering the industry don't see the value of face-to-face learning like the annual conference. They learn differently.

"I believe the younger generation really does want to be involved and make a difference. The discussion should be around how we do it. Millennials are networking online, through Instagram and Snapchat. Associations need to show them the value of meeting with their colleagues in person. Younger people will get involved if we show them what belonging to an association means to them personally."

According to Rutkowski, member engagement is one area in which a low-tech approach is highly successful.

"You cannot underestimate customer service and personalization. People will ignore emails, voicemails...but if you can connect with them on the phone, that makes a difference," Rutkowski says. "I call and talk with two to five members each week. Many are people whom I've never spoken with before. I've been able to get them more involved and to agree to help us through these phone conversations, more than through any other strategy. I personally help them register for events and participate."

Members often quickly recall the event or activity that made them realize the value of the association.

"For many of our members that exact moment was their first NASSTRAC conference," she says. "It was at that conference where they met people like themselves who were struggling with similar challenges. They solved some of their problems listening to excellent speakers or by connecting with individuals who have been where they are now. They realized they were not alone."

To capitalize on this opportunity for bonding, the association offers numerous ways for attendees to connect with colleagues and providers at the annual conference. They organize events such as a newcomer breakfast, an ask-the-expert area for people to receive one-on-one support, and networking receptions. A robust expo hall provides an opportunity for newbies to be introduced to a variety of carriers, third-party logistics companies, and technology providers.

"Often, I hear that the annual conference format for any association is outdated. Folks are too busy, Millennials don't value the face-to-face interaction, etc.," Rutkowski says. "While there needs to be continual rejuvenation, I firmly believe that nothing beats face-to-face networking and interaction with colleagues."

What Association Executives Can Learn From NASSTRAC

1. Manage disruption by planning for it. "You can identify the possibility of major disruptions and construct a response," Rutkowski says. "Having a sound business continuity plan helps. Having tabletop enactments of those disruptions helps even more."

2. Show younger members the value of meeting with colleagues in person. "I firmly believe that nothing beats face-to-face networking and interaction with colleagues," Rutkowski says. "Younger people will get involved if we show them what belonging to an association means to them personally."

3. Don't underestimate customer service and personalization. "I call and talk with two to five members each week. Many are people whom I've never spoken with before," Rutkowski says. "I've been able to get them more engaged and agree to help us through these phone conversations than through any other way. I personally help them register for events and get involved."

4. Make advocacy a priority if your industry is heavily regulated. "We spend a lot of time on federal advocacy, conveying the voice of the shipper and collaborating with other organizations," Rutkowski says. "NASSTRAC collectively communicates shippers' concerns to public policymakers with greater impact and at a lower cost than if each shipper member acted alone."

Food for Thought

· What types of unplanned disruption might your organization experience?
· How can you plan for those events?
· What kinds of member engagement activities are most successful for your organization? Why?
· What could you do to make your interactions with members more personalized?

- What are you doing to engage new members at your annual meeting? Are these strategies working? How could they be improved?

CHAPTER 13: MOVING BEYOND THE TIME CLOCK

Featuring: Stuart Meyer, Former CEO,
National Barbecue & Grilling Association

Overview

Given the national obsession with charred steaks, burgers, and veggies, it's amazing that for decades no single group existed to support the businesses whose professional interests revolve around smoke and flames. The barbecue world was fragmented, with a variety of organizations focused on different segments of this American culinary tradition. The National Barbecue & Grilling Association (NBBQA) was formed to support the growth, expansion, and promotion of the industry across all its branches.

At first glance, NBBQA seems like a mainstream association offering high-quality and high-value programs to its more than 600 members who include restaurateurs, caterers, manufacturers, suppliers and the public at large. In exchange for their membership dollars, NBBQA members receive a portfolio of benefits, including:

- Access to key industry connections across eight special interest groups
- Monthly peer-to-peer learning calls, which are also made available through on-demand audio
- Resources and discounts
- The opportunity to participate in volunteer activities geared toward bringing higher standards and quality control to the industry

NBBQA's Secret Sauce: Virtual Operations

As you might imagine, this organization that represents some of the country's great pit masters has a secret sauce that makes it unique in the association world. NBBQA is a completely virtual workplace. There are no nine-to-five employees and no headquarters. In fact, there isn't any office at all.

Until recently, most associations were staffed by full-time, in-house employees. That model is rapidly changing. Cloud connectivity and apps such as Skype, GoToMeeting and other communications software have made an online-only organization possible. The percentage of workers doing all or some of their work at home increased from 19 percent in 2003 to 24 percent in 2015, according to the Bureau of Labor Statistics. Among those in management, business, financial operations and professional jobs, the percentage is even higher—35 to 38 percent. According to FlexJobs, a company that advertises all types of remote, telecommuting and freelance positions, 68 percent of United States workers say that they expect to work remotely in the future.

Reaching beyond the restrictions of a traditional office environment is becoming more attractive to organizations as they realize the impact on the bottom line as well as on their ability to recruit and maintain top talent. Surprisingly, despite the advantages of a nontraditional workforce, few associations are redefining their organizational structures. In January 2017, FlexJobs released its list of top 100 companies offering telecommuting opportunities. The only association to make this list was the Dallas-based American Heart Association.

To Stuart Meyer, CEO of the National Barbecue & Grilling Association, this news is disheartening. He hasn't worked in an office setting in eight years—including the last two years as CEO of NBBQA. "I serve as a virtual CEO. We are a 100 percent virtual organization," he says.

"Sacred cows are the greatest threat to how we run associations," Meyer notes. "How we define our management and operations practice, and how we work as association executives must evolve rapidly if our organizations are going to continue to be relevant."

According to Meyer, control and trust are the largest barriers to adopting a flexible work environment. "We must stop the punch-clock mentality and the belief that if we let staff out of our sight, they're going to be doing anything other than working.

"It's so easy these days to offer more flexibility through telecommuting and virtual workspaces. The traditional workplace reality is you're lucky if you get up to five hours of productive work out of each employee every day. Commuting, excessive meetings, disruptions and office politics erode productivity." A more fluid organizational structure allows employers to focus staff on activities that play to their strengths rather than the broad responsibilities that typically come with a nine-to-five job. Being open to a remote workforce also means being able to hire the best talent on the market without regard to location.

NBBQA wasn't always so cutting-edge in its approach. Until 2015, the association was run by a traditional management company. That year, the board hired Meyer as interim CEO to help build out an independently run organization. For three months, the board and Meyer worked on defining strategies and priorities for delivering more value to members. Eventually, those decisions led to hiring a four-person team—a CEO, a chief financial officer, an event management planner, and a content editor. These contract employees were all working at different locations. The arrangement was so successful that the need for office space became superfluous.

"If you have members coming to your office regularly, then on some level it makes sense to have a physical space," Meyer points out. "But even in that scenario, it's likely you don't need to have all staff there all the time."

This streamlined organizational structure has allowed Meyer to concentrate on putting an organization that's more than a quarter-century old back into start-up mode. "We have minimal overhead and infrastructure, which has significantly brought down our costs, enabling us to focus more energy on strategic business priorities," Meyer says. Some of the technological solutions that keep this virtual workplace running efficiently include:

- Cloud-based document storage and sharing
- Project management and work collaboration software
- A free conference calling service
- Online shared calendars and deadline tracking
- An advanced VoIP business phone system
- Online media platforms, social media discussion forums, and outsourced specialist partners.

"You have to have certain organizational processes, tools, and structures in place for a remote workforce to work well," Meyer cautions. NBBQA's success is largely attributable to clearly defined procedures, a full suite of technological tools for team collaboration, and a culture of transparency, open communication and accountability.

"Our orientation has been more entrepreneurial with less hierarchical rigidity. There is no intimidation in approaching each other. We have an open dialogue about how we are all performing," Meyer says. "The more institutional constraints and filters you remove, the better the work experience. You don't lose time with people who don't want to talk with each other because of conflict. You create a more conducive environment while offering your team the opportunity to have more freedom and balance in their lives. As we move toward the future, I believe we'll see a continued rise of independent 'fractional' freelance association professionals splitting their time across multiple organizations working on very focused and defined activities and objectives."

This new organizational model also makes creating a high-functioning team a little easier. NBBQA still needs to make tough choices about employees from time to time. "When you have a full-time employee who simply isn't working out for whatever reason, in a traditional setting there is a high standard of care, documentation, and intervention followed by a slow-moving process geared toward performance improvement, tracking and measurement to exhaust all efforts before making what is always a very tough decision. However, as contractors, we are accustomed to working with multiple clients simultaneously on projects and assignments of varying durations. If it isn't working out, the end of a contract term presents a clear option on whether to continue the relationship. These realities enable you to build teams that are aligned with their strengths much faster," Meyer says. "I have found conflict resolution is much easier. I'm giving and receiving real-time feedback through regular and ongoing check-ins as our work relationship is built around very clear and specific tasks, work products and outcomes.

"It's never easy to cut a contractor, but our trade-off is the freedom of a flexible work environment. In this way, we have the agility to find and develop strong performers. That's tough to achieve in the traditional association model with 'catch all' full-time job descriptions that align employees with a mixture of their strengths and weaknesses." Since Meyer became CEO, he's dismissed two contractors. "Team engineering, whether in a traditional sense or with freelancers, requires the right people with the right skill sets, the right strengths, and the right motivation," Meyer says.

Beyond NBBQA's core management team, the organization relies on other support throughout the year. "Just because we process member renewals once a month doesn't mean I need a full-time employee. We outsource this function. We do the same with site selection for conferences," Meyer says. "The art of partnering with other entities and businesses is a big part of the virtual workplace equation. It's about acquiring an agile team of contractors."

Can a Virtual Workplace Be 'Reality' for All Associations?

A virtual, contract-only work environment is a good fit for NBBQA because it's a small organization. "Perhaps if we had a team of 50, we might have a more hierarchal structure. But I think we would still offer flexibility and freedom, so everyone could have true balance in their lives and support things that matter outside their profession," Meyer says.

"If associations fail to keep pace with the constantly accelerating world of work and continue our tradition of lagging behind the corporate world, there could be troubled times ahead," Meyer warns. "Whether it's a virtual environment or a more traditional environment, what's crucial to workplace advancement for associations is realigning how we assemble and use our people.

"Maximum productivity is not the same as optimal productivity. Maximizing the productivity of your employees means you are 'maxing' them out. Reaching the right optimal balance with employees means you are 'optimizing' their productivity. You can create a more efficient and enriching work experience by moving to a more flexible, agile model that better aligns people according to their strengths, so they can make valuable contributions. Virtually—pun intended—anyone can be successful with this model in some shape or form. There are still ways to bring people face-to-face to bond as a team, but not at the frequency or in a setting that can create factions or divisions."

Another critical component for a successful remote workplace is a board that's "on board." Leadership that is focused on micromanaging and control will not respond well to a virtual operating environment.

"What's ultimately better for our associations is separating governance and management," Meyer says. "Association executives must ensure that boards are focused on priority setting. And management must work on the most effective way to support the direction of the board.

"Sometimes, though, you just can't change the reality of how boards operate. Enter the serenity prayer for associations—at some point, accept what you cannot change or control. If you can't get on the same page with your board regarding the operational environment and management of the association, it may be time for a change."

What Association Executives Can Learn From NBBQA

1. Focus on working smarter, not harder. Maximum productivity is not the same as optimum productivity. If you focus on quantity, you run the risk of burning out your employees. "Burn and churn," or high turnover, will only hinder organizational advancement.

2. Control and trust are the largest barriers to adopting a flexible work environment. A board that is accustomed to micromanaging and control will not respond well to virtual operations. If this is your preferred model, either work on evolving the board's mindset or look for another opportunity more aligned with your management philosophy.

3. Moving to an agile workplace model boosts productivity, attracts specialized talent, and reduces operating costs. Associations must have certain organizational processes, tools, and structures in place for a remote workforce to function effectively. NBBQA's success is largely attributable to clear procedures, use of cloud-based management tools for team collaboration, and a culture of transparency, open communication and accountability.

4. Team engineering, whether in a traditional sense or with contractors, requires the right people with the right skill sets, strengths, and motivation. Ensure workers are aligned according to their strengths, have the available resources to do their jobs efficiently and proficiently, and offer a true balance in their lives.

Food for Thought

- Are there virtual workplace strategies that could make your organization operate more efficiently?
- Which aspects of this model appeal to you and which do not? Why?
- Do you think your organization makes the most of your team's strengths?
- If not, what could be done to better align talent with tasks?
- Would your association's board buy into this model? If not, why not?
- How do you think your association's organizational structure will change in the next five years?
- What will the impact of these changes be?

CHAPTER 14: FACING A CHALLENGING ECONOMY WITH BOLD INITIATIVES

Featuring: Dawn Sweeney, CEO, National Restaurant Association and National Restaurant Association Educational Foundation

Overview

In 1917, the Kansas City Restaurant Association boycotted brokers trying to drive up the price of eggs. Ever since, restaurants in the United States have organized to advocate for their businesses and the foodservice industry. Founded in 1919, the National Restaurant Association (NRA) has continued to evolve alongside the needs of its members. Today, the NRA represents a nearly $800 billion industry that employs 14.7 million people. As the association looks forward to celebrating its centennial anniversary it has, at its helm, a CEO who has already significantly advanced the organization through advocacy and innovative programs and services that address the business, social, and nutritional needs of its members, their employees, and the public.

The NRA is the largest trade association in the foodservice sector. The association's mission is straightforward: *We serve our members by advancing and protecting America's restaurant and foodservice industry.* Its history is filled with interesting anecdotes on how it addresses these goals by promoting restaurants and helping to keep them successful, even during the leanest of times. Through Prohibition, the Great Depression, World War II, and, more recently, the recession of

2008, in partnership with state restaurant associations, the NRA has been instrumental in growing the industry via direct marketing and advertising campaigns as well as by supporting member business development. As industry employment has also grown to a staggering 14.7 million, the association has ensured that its members are represented on Capitol Hill and in state houses and cities across the nation on a diverse array of issues, including tip-reporting rules, food policy, business meal deductibility, and labor and employment law.

Over the years, the NRA has been able to mobilize and contribute millions of dollars for community engagement following the 9/11 terrorist attacks and for hurricane relief. As food safety, health, and nutrition have risen in the public consciousness, the association has led the way with food-safety training programs for restaurant employees and initiatives such as Kids Live Well. These activities demonstrate the industry's commitment to helping families and children make healthy choices.

NRA Programs

The NRA provides a wide array of programs and services that support member success:

- Restaurant management: The association advances the effectiveness and professionalism of restaurant management through programs addressing marketing and sales, workforce development, restaurant operations, and food and nutrition.
- Advocacy: Among its many advocacy programs, NRA has created the Kitchen Cabinet, providing local restaurateurs with the tools they need to effectively work with policymakers to support growth and opportunities in their communities.
- Research: Research plays a vital supporting role for the association and its members. Programs include the annual Restaurant Industry Outlook, "What's Hot" Culinary Forecast (conducted in conjunction with the American Culinary Federation), Mapping the Technology Landscape, Restaurant Performance Index, Restaurant Trend Mapper, and many more.
- Events: The annual NRA Show is the largest exhibition in the foodservice industry, attracting more than 65,000 attendees each year. NRA also offers a wide variety of educational programming, not only at the annual show, but also through webinars, summits and executive study groups.

- Public Relations: The association actively promotes the industry and the positive impact it makes through its public relations programs such as America Works Here, Kids Live Well, and Fighting Hunger.
- Workforce Development: Through support of its education foundation, the association is actively engaged with students and educators building awareness of careers in foodservice and providing them with information, hands-on experiences, and scholarships. In addition, the foundation supports military personnel transitioning to the private sector, as well as opportunities for youth looking for their first job.

NRA by the Numbers:

- $116 million revenue in 2016
- 97 percent of revenue from non-dues programs and services
- 52 state restaurant association partners (all 50 states plus Washington, DC and Puerto Rico)
- 330 employees, with offices in Washington, DC; Chicago, IL; Lansing, MI; Orlando, FL; and Providence, RI

The Search for a Life that Matters

Relationships, work, service to others, health, and, of course, food! These are the things that contribute to lives well lived and the things Dawn Sweeney has nurtured in her work as CEO of the NRA. Under Sweeney's leadership, not surprisingly, the NRA has grown because she brought her impressive track record for expansion and entrepreneurship to the association. What was unexpected, perhaps to no one more than Sweeney, is the all-encompassing opportunity she has had to make a tangible difference in the lives of so many restaurateurs, foodservice workers, American children, and the public at-large.

Sweeney is a career association professional. She has contributed her considerable marketing, advocacy, and policy experience to the National Rural Electric Cooperative Association, the International Dairy Foods Association, and immediately prior to joining the NRA, to AARP. Sweeney's career at AARP included serving as the association's group executive officer for membership and later president and CEO of AARP Services, a wholly-owned for-profit subsidiary of AARP. At AARP, Sweeney led the development of products and services, including the launch of AARP Financial, which effectively quadrupled the company's revenues to nearly $800 million.

In 2007 Sweeney was lured away from AARP to take on a new challenge. "I was approached by the NRA board to help them benchmark the skills they were looking for in their new CEO. I wasn't interviewing for the position. I just met them for dinner and we talked," Sweeney says. "Then they asked if we could meet again. They were all CEOs and C-level executives of restaurant companies—enormously engaging, fun, energetic entrepreneurs. They told me they were looking to make transformational change.

Sweeney was happy at AARP and with the clear contributions she and her colleagues were making to the organization and to the lives of older Americans. Yet through her interviews with the NRA board search committee, Sweeney saw that the restaurant industry could be a catalyst for social change. She just needed to roll up her sleeves and figure out how to get it done.

When Sweeney joined the NRA in 2007, the food culture in the United States was thriving and so was the restaurant business. The industry was then, as it is today, a significant contributor to U.S. GDP and one of the largest private sector employers. NRA had annual revenues of about $50 million, but Sweeney knew this did not represent the organization's full capability. The question was: How could that potential be realized?

"Fifty percent of the people in this country have worked in a restaurant, but unfortunately for me, I was not one of them!" explains Sweeney. "So, the first year I was on the job, I probably worked in 15 restaurants for a day or two at a time. I worked the drive-through. I did food prep. I was a hostess. I tended bar, and I worked in the executive offices. This was the best way for me to get a quicker and deeper understanding of the industry." She gained empathy and insight. "Working in the restaurants was the most fabulous way to get a sense of the demographics, stories, and backgrounds of the people. It was an enormously powerful part of my training."

Then in 2008, after 19 years of consecutive growth, the Great Recession hit the United States economy hard. Sweeney was prepared. She understood that opportunity lay in helping the industry weather the storm. The NRA had historical experience leading its members through both good and challenging economic times. Sweeney and her team knew what their members needed.

"One of the first things I learned coming from a very large organization like AARP to a trade association is that there is no room for making a (big) mistake. You must really think through the essence of the scope and scale of what you are doing. We developed products and services for an industry experiencing extreme challenges."

Although membership grew during the recession as restaurant owners were searching for coping strategies, dues were not the answer to helping members or the association through the economic downturn. Sweeney understood that instead of retracting during the recession, she had to be proactive and fill industry needs. Programs and services had to grow. Building on a firm base of existing initiatives, the association launched a health insurance offering customized to the restaurant industry, expanded its food safety programs, supported advanced credit card processing, grew the trade show, and engaged more actively in advocacy. The industry and the association emerged from the recession stronger than ever and have continued to grow. NRA increased its annual revenue from $50 million in 2007 to $116 million in 2016.

Sweeney says there is still so much to do. "Today, we are increasingly focused on advocacy. We see where the world is going. We can get ahead of the curve when it comes to addressing challenges like public health and workforce development."

Providing health care to restaurant workers and ensuring an adequate supply of workers, many of whom are immigrants, continues to be a challenge. Health care and immigration reform have been top White House agenda items for the last four administrations, so NRA has had to develop strategies to cope with changing perspectives on the issues that are of vital importance to the success of their members.

"You have to pivot," Sweeney says. "You find other ways to engage in your agenda. You take advantage of opportunities presented and become flexible." And, you take a nonpartisan approach. "You find the people who have the values you can align with and make the most of the opportunities there. We can count on working with people on both sides of the aisle. You have to be able to work with whomever will work with you to make positive change."

Sweeney's advocacy for others is not focused only on the restaurant industry but extends to the association management community and women in the profession. Like many women, Sweeney is not particularly motivated by money or title, but is driven by making a positive impact. While she has attained high levels of all three of these achievements in her career, she says the first two have been the unintended consequence of the transformations that she strives to make.

Still, Sweeney is acutely aware that pay equity is an issue that the association industry needs to address. Men leading smaller associations can make more money than their female counterparts leading larger organizations. Sweeney has broken through the ranks to be one of the few women among the highest paid association CEOs. This wasn't just a happy circumstance related to the job she has done. She intentionally worked with her compensation committee to break the pattern for the association industry. Based on the size and the scope of the organization, she knew what she should be paid and made an objective case that was based in facts.

"I have never felt I have been given less of an opportunity because I am a woman, although I do believe this was true for previous generations of women," Sweeney notes. By claiming her rightful place among the ranks of the highest paid association CEOs, Sweeney has created a precedent for both women employed by NRA and those she inspires in the association community, to be a part of the rising tide.

For all she has accomplished, Sweeney is most grateful for the professional opportunities she has had throughout her career and especially her relationships in the restaurant industry—with which she is so proud and grateful to be associated.

"The restaurant business is one of the hardest industries in which to make a living. People in this sector work so hard. They just keep trying. They keep reaching out to find people who are willing to share their experiences, and they help each other to be successful. People in this industry are really kind to one another. I found my place here."

What Association Executives Can Learn From the NRA

1. The path to growth is empathy. In a world in which we increasingly see our members and customers as data, Sweeney still takes the time to get to know those she serves personally, and it has made all the difference in her career. "My affinity for people is what has led to my success," Sweeney says. "I show up and listen, I get all the information needed to know what to do next. I look for pain points." This personal approach creates an intimate knowledge of your constituents, resulting in the ability to develop products and services that meet their needs, drive customer engagement, and ultimately engender loyalty.

2. Build where you already have residency. There is no magic formula for growth. Expansion is not just about new products to address new markets, it's also about building on your core competencies and expanding current programs to engage a wider audience of participants. The NRA had a successful food safety program for managers that has expanded to include other restaurant employees—growing the market from 1 million restaurant managers to several million restaurant employees. According to Sweeney, if you already have a model for success, you just need to put arms and legs on it.

3. Know your worth. It is easy to be satisfied with your salary when you reap many other benefits from your work. It is important, however, to know your worth and make sure the people involved in making compensation decisions that affect

you do as well. As Sweeney says, it's your responsibility to "stick up for yourself, advocate for your team, and lead the way for the next generation."

4. Engage in philanthropy outside of work. Years ago, when Sweeney was at AARP, she made a personal decision to become involved as a board member of Save the Children. "I have learned so much, in terms of leadership and management, through participation in outside boards, but more importantly I feel more well-rounded," Sweeney says. "I have been able to expand my impact in new and different ways and use my intellectual and creative skills to contribute to true global and humanitarian progress. I truly believe that some of my greatest leadership lessons have come from helping others unravel complex problems. I return to my 'day job' with new skills and perspectives that ultimately benefit our organization and the restaurant industry."

Food for Thought

- What are your organization's core competencies? How could you grow those initiatives into new products and services?
- How could your association face an economic downturn proactively? What could your association deliver that members might need during a challenging situation?
- How could you bring greater empathy to your role as a leader?
- How does your organization impact the well-being of members? Are there ways to extend these benefits?

CHAPTER 15: GAME-CHANGING TRANSPORTATION AND ASSOCIATION MANAGEMENT

Featuring: David Schutt, Ph.D., CEO, SAE Group

Overview

Three years before the Ford Model T rolled off production lines in 1908 and reshaped the American landscape, the Society of Automobile Engineers (SAE) was formed. The goal was to expand a shared vision and enhance collaboration among professionals working on technical design problems and engineering standards. The organization attracted individuals with a common interest in advancing the fledgling discipline of automobile engineering.

It wasn't long before game-changing industry leaders, including Thomas Edison and Orville Wright, realized that transportation engineering societies could benefit from pooling their expertise and working together. During World War I, as aircraft production was being accelerated, the organization made a subtle name change, replacing automobile with automotive, thus embracing engineers working on all forms of self-propelled vehicles.

One hundred years later, the SAE Group is at the forefront of a great technological leap. Their work on the launch of autonomous vehicles is certain to create seismic changes in both our work and leisure habits.

SAE Group Organizations

- **SAE Group** is a consortium of nonprofit organizations and for-profit companies managed collectively to serve stakeholders in the mobility industry. Members represent aerospace, automotive, and commercial vehicles.
- **SAE International** is the flagship organization in the SAE Group. It is a professional association offering continuing education and networking to more than 128,000 members. SAE International serves the industry through the development of technical standards and lifelong learning to advance the engineering of mobility systems.
- **The Performance Review Institute** is a trade association that develops performance standards and quality assurance, accreditation, and certification programs. Its main initiatives are industry-managed audit programs advancing the aerospace (Nadcap) as well as the Transportation and Power Generation (TPG) and medical device (MedAccred) industries. It also manages a registrar program for general quality systems.
- **The SAE Industry Technology Consortia** functions as a trade association servicing the automotive, aerospace and commercial vehicle sectors through standards development and the provision of a forum for collaboration to solve technical issues. ITC is also responsible for managing the Defense Automotive Technologies Consortia.
- **Defense Automotive Technologies Consortia** (DATC) facilitates the development and transition of advanced automotive technologies to military and government agencies. Members of DATC are from private industry, nonprofit organizations, and academia. Technologies addressed include: automotive cybersecurity, vehicle safety technologies, vehicle light weighting, autonomous vehicles and intelligent systems, connected vehicles, advanced energy storage technologies, propulsion technologies, and active suspension technologies.

SAE Group by the Numbers:

- 4 separately incorporated not-for-profit organizations and five for-profit subsidiaries and joint ventures
- Network of more than 128,000 professional members
- 8 office locations around the world: North America (5), Europe (2) and Asia (1)

- 400+ employees
- $150+ million annual revenue

Once Again...History in the Making

David Schutt, CEO of SAE Group, appreciates the unique position of the businesses he serves. Unlike many standards organizations, SAE International does not simply reflect the industries it represents: it advances them. Developing standards for autonomous vehicles has placed his organizations among the pioneers who are bringing this revolutionary new transportation to market. "It is an incredibly complex process," Schutt says. "There is an amazing amount of technology involved. Production has to be standardized for it to become cost competitive but not too quickly that it thwarts innovation." SAE International has already been successful establishing classifications for on-road vehicles that have been widely adopted, including by the National Highway Traffic Safety Administration (NHTSA) for use in its Federal Automated Vehicles Policy.

Not surprisingly, the more autonomous a vehicle becomes, the more standards are needed to address the risks related to safety and cybersecurity. As an example, Schutt says, "We must develop protocols for securing and locking down a vehicle. The original equipment manufacturers used to keep control of everything, but now a single vehicle is just one node on a very complex network. That's the reality of what the car is becoming," Schutt says. The automotive industry is not alone in trying to address an increasingly connected world that is larger than the sum of its parts. Technologies are braided, and where one begins and another ends is becoming difficult to decipher. "Aerospace is going through similar issues," according to Schutt. "Someone's going to find a way to connect the cockpit network and the Wi-Fi network. You've got a large attack surface there for cyber criminals." These are the sorts of challenges that SAE must anticipate and address.

Adding to the complexity of developing standards to secure vehicles that are as yet untried on a mass scale is the imperative of keeping up with local and national regulations. Players in the regulatory arena in the United States alone include the NHTSA, as well as state departments of motor vehicles. The municipal governments of the world's largest cities are also impacting mobility industries. "What we're seeing is city mayors having far more influence over the future of urban transportation than ever before," says Schutt. SAE International must operate from a broad perspective to develop standards that can conform to current and future regulations at the international, national, regional, and local levels.

Although SAE Group has public safety as a key focus, standards also affect business competitiveness. For instance, how do you address cybersecurity from a business perspective? How do you drive standards development in a globally competitive environment? "If we do it right, we can manifest these technologies more quickly and effectively," Schutt says. Speed to market, return on investment, and value creation are all enabled by industries coming together to create harmonious standards that advance manufacturing while ensuring public safety and environmental sustainability.

Given the number of players in this industry, Schutt sees collaboration as an important ingredient for success. He believes that nonprofits must learn how to work together far better than they have in the past. "Those who want to fight over a shrinking pie—I let them go for it. I'm not interested," Schutt says. "If there is an information product, a marketplace, or a customer base of use to both of us, then let's find ways to partner and make it commercially viable."

Achieving and Sustaining Preferred Provider Status

Schutt, a chemical physicist, came into his role at SAE Group having worked in several executive positions for the American Chemical Society, including the chief financial officer and chief strategy officer. Shortly after joining SAE as CEO, the Great Recession hit the automotive, aerospace, and commercial vehicles industries hard. "When I first came in 2008, our organization went from $60 million to $40 million overnight. I had to reduce our workforce by a third," Schutt recalls.

While this was difficult for all concerned, the recession allowed Schutt to reconceive the organization starting at the top. He turned over the entire executive team and brought in leaders from the commercial sector who were ready to both compete and collaborate to support growth. He divested and outsourced processes and activities that were outside the organization's core competencies. This allowed the group to focus acutely on what they do best. He forged new partnerships and made acquisitions to grow marketing, products, and workforce.

Another key structural change was to reframe the roles of volunteers, creating a more meaningful and effective experience. "We engage more than 10,000 engineers worldwide. You can never have enough volunteers. Because what we are doing is so industry-critical, they find the time to help us. Their employers support them. But the volunteer workforce doesn't have time or the professional expertise to direct or manage our operations. We need them as market perspective and technical support."

Making SAE Group as innovative as the industries it represents also required updating the International governance structure. Schutt worked with the board to move away from what he describes as the "1950s representative model" to a small and nimble team of leaders selected to serve for their expertise rather than their geographical location. Competency-based boards, which bring together trendsetters in their industries, can be more intellectually challenging to work with. Schutt finds this to be both stimulating and productive for the organization. "I'd rather debate with 12 bright people and lose than work with a board that simply defers to my judgment," Schutt says.

The same philosophy of expansion that facilitated the group's rebound from the recession has led to year-over-year expansion. Today, SAE International alone has grown its topline revenue to more than $85 million (2015), a more than 50 percent increase over pre-recession operating revenue, making it the largest contributor to the $150 million+ SAE Group. When asked whether this growth was the result of strategy or opportunity, Schutt replies, "I consider myself to be a strategist, so I like to think what I am doing has an impact. I like to think strategy has led to growth, but it is also opportunistic. I didn't create the recession, but I took advantage of it."

Schutt is clearly a member of an emerging group of growth leaders serving associations today. He has the good fortune to be part of an exciting industry that is both shrinking the globe and reaching for the stars. He strives to make SAE an organization whose operations and management reflect its position at the forefront of the transportation network.

What Association Executives Can Learn From SAE Group

1. Learn to collaborate. The SAE Group is built on a foundation of cross-industry, globe-spanning collaboration. Collaboration has become a part of the DNA of the organization, and it is what allows it to be nimble enough to keep up with the pace of change in technology-driven industries.
2. Understand your organization's unique value. The organizations within the SAE Group are dedicated to serving their missions. Schutt, however, takes a nontraditional perspective regarding their roles vis-à-vis industry. "We're another trusted supplier to the automotive and aerospace industries for what we do: standards, technical content, conferences, and professional development. We just get to do it with a not-for-profit tax status." Trade and professional associations can offer unique benefits to the corporations they serve, but they must prove their worth by meeting market needs. Successful associations

deliver high-quality products and perform services—at competitive prices—that are not available elsewhere. Business is changing at an unprecedented rate, and associations must keep the pace. This may mean developing a new business model, updating the way products and services are delivered, or even rethinking the definition of a customer. Existing core competencies may need to be enhanced and new core competencies acquired.

3. Focus volunteers on where they add value. It takes a battalion of engineers to address the volume, complexity, and critical impact of the standards SAE Group organizations are developing. This is where they add value and how they best serve the industry. Ensuring that volunteer leaders and staff respect each other's roles is critical to organizational growth and vitality. Lines can get blurred little by little. Committee chairs take on administrative responsibility. Board members question the organizational direction and dive into operations instead of addressing their trust issue. Staff find it easier to do committee work than to work with the committee to better accomplish its tasks. Crossover in volunteer and staff functions creates confusion and an inability to address market opportunities when they arise. Learning to effectively blend these complementary roles enables an association to perform at the highest level.

4. Be a learning organization. Be a part of a learning industry. Artificial intelligence in autonomous cars is designed to mimic the human brain. Instead of trying to hard code responses to every conceivable situation, engineers create algorithms that allow the vehicles to "learn." The true power of artificial intelligence, however, is that it can be shared with other vehicles in real time, improving a whole fleet's ability to navigate roads. Schutt sees his organizations as a similar learning system. They make mistakes but learn as they go. He extends this thinking to the association industry. "I think we are all 'dumb' cars initially, but what we've got to do is learn from one another. The whole association community has to go to the next level or else we are all stuck."

Food for Thought

- Does your association engage in regulating or developing industry standards?
- If so, what challenges and benefits come from this activity?
- If not, would there be any benefit to being more active in this arena?
- What would the impact of having to downsize be on your organization? How could you make the most of a difficult situation?

- Are you using volunteers effectively? What are you doing well? What needs improvement?
- Are your board members selected based on skills and experience, geography, or some combination of the two? What are the advantages in moving toward a more competence-based leadership? What are the obstacles to choosing that path?

CHAPTER 16: MAKING CRITICAL CONNECTIONS

Featuring: David Martin, CAE, CEO and Executive Vice President, Society of Critical Care Medicine

Overview

Members of the Society of Critical Care Medicine (SCCM) hold lives in their hands. The Society represents nearly 16,000 critical care professionals in more than 100 countries. These dedicated workers provide close, constant watch over the more than 5.7 million patients who are admitted annually to intensive care units or trauma centers in the United States. The demand for their services is increasing rapidly due to longer life expectancy, an expanding aging population, and improvements in the delivery of health care.

SCCM Data: Its Value Adds Up

When David Martin became CEO of SCCM in 2001, the organization, which was located in Anaheim, California, had experienced a wide range of operational and financial challenges. Under Martin's leadership, SCCM has more than doubled its membership and tripled revenues. He also revitalized the organization, transforming it into a technological leader by providing an unprecedented level of communication and information management services.

Making Data-driven Decisions

To quickly obtain information on the status of important activities such as event registration, member counts or the progress of shipped products, staff relies on integrated dashboards. These up-to-the-minute data allow them to easily make operational adjustments to positively affect the ultimate outcome.

Requiring Technology Skills

Martin stays current on technology and expects staff to do the same. He hires employees with both quantitative and collaborative skills.

Developing a Technology Strategy

Martin and his team at SCCM have been early adopters of technology and data-driven decision making. Shortly after the relocation of SCCM headquarters to the Chicago area, the organization's leadership developed an information technology plan and began to implement it in a measured, phased approach. Everyone realized it was a long-term endeavor, but one that was vitally important.

The first phase of the plan merged disparate databases containing customer records. Today, the "single database rule" still applies and is contained in society policy. All information on customers is linked to a single source record, regardless of what system is used to manage or generate those data. This enables staff and the Society's elected leadership to better understand member needs and activities and also provides members/customers with an improved experience.

In 2007, SCCM embarked on a mission to go paperless. The office transferred all paper records into an electronic document management system. As the SCCM headquarters was moving into a newly owned building, it was an ideal time to reduce space needs by eliminating paper file storage. It also had the benefit of putting records, formerly contained in file storage rooms, at employees' fingertips for rapid response to member or leadership needs.

SCCM was one of the early adopters of website responsive design, which allowed the organization to automatically detect whether a user was accessing the site through a PC or smartphone browser and provide the appropriate view. The mobile version of its website contained fewer graphics for faster access, and content was streamlined to focus on the association's most recent updates and news. The new websites were also equipped with sign-in functions for both members and nonmembers to access large online libraries of SCCM-created content.

One of the technology goals was to link and centrally connect all data sources— bringing together customer transactions, committee assignments, email communications, website and other more traditional data types. This unification made it possible to build customer personas and uncover new insights concerning their constituents' needs. Mapping the data sources and linking them to analytic tools gave management the ability to review every aspect of SCCM's operation, both historically and in real time. This process also facilitated the development of a sophisticated customer engagement index. The system provides a real-time score for each of its 175,000 customers. Customers also see the results, so they can compare themselves to their peers.

"Going 100 percent digital allowed us to get a 360-degree view of our constituents," Martin says. "SCCM can focus investment in its most important customers, see patterns in demographics and respond with changes in pricing or adjustments in strategies.

"The data results in business intelligence that better meets customer needs," Martin explains. "The data we collect and analyze provides new ways of thinking about customers that drive revenue growth in the short term and create insight into future behaviors and new product development in the long term."

"Regular, proactive maintenance to keep data clean is required," says Martin, also noting that establishing appropriate data security is vital. "In this day and age, security needs to be set up properly to protect your valuable information, but at the same time, staff must have easy access to make appropriate decisions. This balance is always the biggest challenge for management."

Preparing for a Crisis

SCCM has a long history of responding to emergencies of all kinds, including natural disasters, wars, and terrorist attacks. To better prepare his association to face the unexpected, Martin introduced routine training drills and scenarios outlining how the organization would respond in a disaster. This groundwork paid off when Hurricane Katrina made it impossible for SCCM to hold its 2006 annual meeting in New Orleans. Staff implemented an emergency response plan, and the event took place at an alternative destination with few challenges. The organization responds with the same efficiency when a disaster occurs far from headquarters and the world needs trained medical personnel. When an earthquake struck Haiti in 2010, just as

SCCM's annual meeting was coming to a close, they were ready and able to provide aid.

Before remote work became a more commonplace selling point for workforce talent and workplace efficiencies, SCCM was already testing virtual office operations. In 2009, during the onset of the swine flu (H1N1) pandemic, SCCM prepared for the possibility that its headquarters operations could be impacted if the disease took root in Chicago. It was possible that public health officials would isolate individuals in their homes until the crisis passed.

The association developed a remote operations plan to accommodate the need for both a short-term and longer-term headquarters absence while still providing its full range of member services. Although the pandemic ended up not being as severe as feared, SCCM's Remote Operations Mode was put to actual use during the blizzard of February 2011.

All systems operated according to plan, and the full staff was connected and provided services remotely. They could collaborate and access the association management database and business monitoring dashboards and even operate the switchboard from their off-site locations. They also could access security cameras and other monitoring systems that report on power, temperature, humidity, and additional facility operations. These activities, which are important to the building's safety, continue functioning even in the event of a power failure thanks to backup power generators.

During a longer-term event, such as a pandemic, SCCM's Remote Operations Mode calls for designated staff to visit headquarters on a schedule in which they do not encounter other colleagues. This permits a physical inspection and maintenance of the building, collection and redistribution of mail to home addresses as necessary, and other tasks that would benefit from a physical presence at the building.

Point, Click, Care

Innovation is not only part of the SCCM staff culture, it is routinely called upon by members of SCCM in their practice of critical care.

Some intensive care unit (ICU) patients cannot easily communicate with physicians and nurses because life-supporting equipment prevents their ability to speak or due to language barriers. In 2013, a group of enterprising SCCM physicians sought out a programmer to develop an app with a graphical interface to help these patients have a voice in their care.

SCCM negotiated a private label agreement with the original member creators of the app, who used a moderate investment by SCCM to make upgrades. Over the course of six months and several iterations, new features were implemented and tested, culminating in the app's release in fall of 2013. Since then, patients have been using it to indicate where they are feeling pain and to alert caregivers when they are thirsty, having trouble breathing or experiencing other discomfort. It also displays common questions and concerns in 19 languages, two of which are shown on-screen at a time.

"We were told before what we do at SCCM headquarters helps with patient care. But with this app, we help at the point of care," Martin says.

Following this positive experience, SCCM launched an App Challenge to drive innovation further and harness the creative power of their group. Members were invited to submit a smartphone app of their own design or a new idea they thought would be useful.

Many ICU providers are embracing sophisticated electronic systems that connect ICU patient data to critical care specialists at remote locations. These medical professionals provide real-time monitoring, diagnostic, and intervention services in conjunction with bedside staff. In selected settings, telemedicine—also called tele-ICU or e-ICU—care has shortened the duration of ICU stays and reduced the ICU mortality rate, which may translate into lower hospital costs and better use of resources. "For some patients, having diagnostic and treatment decisions made from remote locations means receiving assistance from professionals who have higher levels of training and expertise," Martin says.

Hospitals, where SCCM members work, are still trying to convert to more robust and interconnected electronic health management systems. According to Martin: "While this may place a strain on the workforce, it is good for patients and should continue."

Further, technology tools in the ICU, such as handheld and bedside ultrasound equipment, are changing rapidly. "Members need to know how to use these instruments and embrace the opportunity to have more information at the bedside," Martin says.

SCCM has proved that the better you know your customers, the more you will be able to provide services that are uniquely tailored to meet their needs and to extend your association's reach. Data and technology are powerful tools that can be leveraged to deliver impactful service.

"At SCCM, we have ventured into new areas such as quality improvement collaborations, basic research initiatives, data registries, and others," Martin says. "They are all new and developing but hold the promise that associations can do more than just their traditional activities."

What Association Executives Can Learn From SCCM

1. Tie digital strategies to your business goals. Determine how your digital efforts will help achieve organizational goals. Where do you begin? First, identify and gather current data assets: Which data are stored in the association management system (AMS), what third-party vendor data can be integrated into existing systems, and what external resources can be mapped? Then apply and align your information to specific organizational goals.

2. Know your audience. Your audience engagement cycle should be to listen, plan, build, engage, analyze—and repeat. Analytics won't have meaning until you identify your entire customer base: who they are, where they live, their digital habits, interests, preferences and goals. For instance, using IP addresses for website visits can enable an association to personalize information on a local or regional basis, making it a better user experience.

3. Establish a culture of knowledge management. Discuss the importance of managing knowledge and information both implicitly and tacitly. Hire those who know analytics and data well; key members of your team should be sharing knowledge across the organization to diminish silos, improve efficiencies and drive business results. Analytics from different business units will help guide priorities. For example, if email click-through rates are satisfactory, but conversion to registration is low, consider whether the issue lies with the registration system. Where in the conversion funnel are prospects dropping?

4. Harness big data to continually improve and provide better service. Associations have the benefit of being mission driven, motivating volunteers to elevate their professions to improve the world. Big data plays an important role in associations that are a key supplier of education and professional development, which leads to mission achievements. Through data, associations can harvest new insights about customers, the profession and their competition in order to thrive and be a highly effective organization.

Food for Thought

- Could your association benefit from greater centralization and integration of data?

- Are you using your members' innovative capabilities to create new products and services and expand your organization's reach?
  - Are your analytics and other data being shared across departments?
  - Does your organization have a robust disaster plan in place?

CHAPTER 17: BIBLICAL MARKETING SPARKS ENGAGEMENT AND INNOVATION

Featuring: Robert Voltmann, President and CEO, Transportation Intermediaries Association

Overview

Members of the Transportation Intermediaries Association (TIA) are movers and shakers. They operate in a high-risk environment that demands scrupulous attention to detail and constant adaption to unforeseen circumstances. TIA represents the third-party logistics companies (3PLs) across North America. These organizations help their customers transport products efficiently and effectively around the globe. They are supply chain savants who are experts at shipping everything from appliances to auto parts over the rails, through the air, and across the ocean. Traditionally, 3PLs worked with other providers to route goods to their ultimate destination. Today, many 3PLs have expanded their services beyond routing to include direct transport, packaging, warehousing and inventory control.

Although 3PLs are a big business with a low public profile, almost every manufacturing shipper uses their services to move products. They represent a $160 billion industry that is growing at two to three times the rate of the U.S. gross domestic product and employs 126,000 workers, with an annual payroll of $7.5 billion.

Founded in 1978, TIA's staff of 18 provides traditional trade association services to its 1,600 member companies, which tend to be small to medium size enterprises,

90 percent of which are family-based businesses. TIA's objective is to help 3PLs "better manage their companies for growth and profit." The association provides:

- Protection of member interests through active lobbying
- Education, research, and networking opportunities to develop CEOs and their staff
- Products and services that are available to advance member companies
- High ethical standards in the industry
- Industry best practices
- Promotion of member companies

Delivering Value Through Political and Personal Advocacy

When Bob Voltmann joined TIA as CEO, he had a plan. He would put the organization on a growth path and move on. Twenty years later, Voltmann is still at the helm, or as he puts it, in his "tenth two-year assignment." During the last two decades, he has grown TIA revenue from $750,000 to more than $6 million in short sprints. He has also worked to protect his members' brands and improve the overall reputation of the transportation industry.

A booming transportation industry creates a fertile environment for continued 3PL growth; however, expansion is dependent on improving supply chain security. Operating worldwide in high-risk environments, 3PLs are vulnerable to carrier fraud such as fictitious pickup and driver identity theft. While digital communications have improved efficiency, technology can also make it difficult to detect criminal components. This is especially true in a "deregulated" industry. Under Voltmann's leadership, TIA takes proactive measures to combat fraud and secure the positive reputation of its members and their customers.

Combatting Fraud

Working with the American Trucking Association and the Owner Operators Independent Drivers Association, in 2012, TIA lobbied for federal legislation that would help fight fraud in the transportation industry. Commercial carriers hauling cargo in interstate commerce must be registered with the Federal Motor Carrier

Safety Administration and must have a U.S. Department of Transportation identifier number and, in many cases, have an Interstate Authority to Operate or MC number.

While the federal legislation was a step in the right direction, enforcement has been an issue. "Every game has to have rules. Even a deregulated industry must have rules," Voltmann says. Unfortunately, the federal agency charged with enforcement has challenges, he adds.

Therefore, TIA is also proactive in providing services to its members that enhance their security. Specifically, TIA offers:

- Bond services at two levels providing assurance to 3PL customers that TIA members adhere to the highest levels of professional standards.
- Watchdog service informing all members to review reports of carrier problems and fraud.
- Model contracts that provide legal protection.
- Frameworks outlining guidance on combatting fraud.
- Discounts on theft protection and recovery products.

Tackling Disruption

While TIA remains vigilant about protecting its members, their customers, and the public against illegal and unethical practices in the transportation and logistics industry, today the organization faces new challenges.

"We are looking at a huge disruption in our marketplace related to digitization, like everyone else," Voltmann says. "Our people help manufacturers manage capacity using road, rail, and air. But technology is going to do that in the future."

The impact technology will have on members is hard to predict, but TIA is working to discern how current trends are prescient to the future. "We watch what Amazon and Uber are doing in this space. If blockchain is successful, it will take away another part of what our members do," Voltmann says. "We are proactively trying to help our members figure out how not to become commoditized." Blockchain allows digital ledgers consisting of transaction "blocks" to be shared across computer networks. There is no central authority and therefore no way to tamper with the records. Since 3PLs process financial transactions, blockchain is likely to have a significant impact. But just as TIA has not hesitated to fight fraud, it's tackling, head on, potential disruptions being caused by this software. The organization is convening members to discuss the impact of Blockchain and other innovations as well as to consider how the industry can advance along with technology.

Much like Voltmann himself, most TIA members are excited by progress and change. "Our members are scrappers. Many created something out of nothing," Voltmann says. TIA members are very collaborative, learning and engaging not only with each other but with industry partners, too. While many associations struggle to get participants to the trade show floor, TIA members line up to speak to exhibitors who can potentially make their businesses more efficient and effective.

Knowing that the industry is collaborative by both nature and necessity, Voltmann has a unique philosophy regarding traveling to meet members, prospective members, and potential partners. He calls it "biblical marketing"—sending TIA evangelists out across the country. TIA staff meets face-to-face with a significant portion of its members each year, either at their various corporate offices or at small gatherings. "We, as a staff, attended 56 events last year," Voltmann says. "We talk to members and prospects and ask them what excites them and what keeps them awake at night."

While some executives of small associations limit the number of public appearances to those they can personally handle, Voltmann has complete confidence in his staff to represent the organization. It is the only way TIA can be everywhere it needs to be. Voltmann has a particular employee profile. "They are all disruptors. They didn't quite fit where they were because their associations always wanted to keep doing things the way they were doing them."

So why has Voltmann stayed on at TIA all these years? "It is a challenge. There is always disruption, but we are growing. It's fun," Voltmann says. It is clear, that instead of turning his back on change, Voltmann is energized by the constant course corrections needed to navigate his industry's shifting landscape. He's excited to help his members greet the unexpected and succeed as a 4.0 association.

What Association Executives Can Learn From TIA

1. Break it down. Although Voltmann has always had a long-term vision for his organization, he has approached his work as CEO as a series of short-term assignments. This creates focus and keeps him engaged in the work and with his members. It also makes it possible for him and the organization to be more fearless tackling tough problems. Finally, it allows for course correction if the path the organization is following proves to be slightly off course.
2. Embrace a challenge. Whether working to improve the security of the industry or to redefine the market based on new technology such as Blockchain, Voltmann does not shy away from a challenge. This attitude is vital to growth

and keeps an association from stalling once it has reached a mature state. Addressing challenges continually breathes new life into organizations, keeps them close to those they serve, and advances the mission. This proactive approach often involves taking calculated risks. Scenario planning, whether formal or informal, can help an organization visualize the impact of various responses and support effective and informed new ventures.

3. Get out of the office...a lot. One of the biggest challenges CEOs face is isolation. Voltmann makes it a point to be out in the industry. He meets frequently with his members, prospects, partners, potential collaborators, and even on occasion his members' customers. There are no walls that surround Voltmann. This keeps him engaged and approachable and helps spur innovation at TIA.

4. Know your type. Voltmann is clear on the characteristics of potential staff members with whom he will work well. He looks for disruptors and innovators who may not fit into the traditional association environment. He seeks out people who can be collaborators and can be trusted to represent the interests of the association. Voltmann is attuned to talent, scoping individuals for later hire when the opportunities present themselves. As a result, hiring staff is an easier process and they tend to be more successful in the organization.

Food for Thought

- Could you break down your association's long-term vision into short-term assignments? Would that be a beneficial approach for you? For your staff? For your members? If not, why not?
- What challenges to your organization/members are not being addressed? Why are these issues being ignored? What could you do to put them on the agenda?
- Do you and your senior staff interact regularly with members who are not in leadership positions? Can you accurately describe your membership demographics? Could you develop a profile of member wants/needs in each demographic group?
- What personality traits do you look for when you hire staff? Why are these qualities important to you? To the organization?

CHAPTER 18: POWERING INNOVATION

Featuring: Mark Thorsby,
former Executive Vice President, Battery Council
International and Vice President of Consulting
Services, SmithBucklin Corporation*

Overview

In the race to protect the environment, one of the biggest winners is an unlikely contender. The lead battery, a commonplace product that is over 150 years old, is a recycling marvel. According to a National Recycling Rate Study commissioned by the Battery Council International (BCI), 99.1 percent of all battery lead is recycled. When you compare that to 55 percent of aluminum soft drink and beer cans, 45 percent of newspapers, and 26 percent of glass bottles, in spite of their long product history, lead batteries take on an impressive modernity.

As the nonprofit trade association representing the industry, BCI is focused on maintaining an innovative orientation towards both products and services. Previously led by Mark Thorsby, executive vice president and vice president of consulting services at SmithBucklin, the association strives to inspire its members to maintain cutting-edge initiatives in an increasingly competitive climate. Lead battery manufacturers and recyclers, marketers and retailers, suppliers of raw materials and equipment, and consultants are all included under the organization's umbrella.

An incredibly versatile product, lead batteries provide power for both utilitarian tasks and heavy-duty entertainment. They are the spark that brings machines from lawn mowers to golf carts and snowmobiles to life. They also make possible the "start-stop" vehicle control systems that are helping manufacturers meet Corporate Average Fuel Economy (CAFE) standards and reduce emissions. Additionally, critical service providers such as cell phone towers, hospitals, and data storage servers rely on lead batteries for backup power.

The lead battery industry is the world's largest consumer of lead, yet in keeping with its environmentally friendly profile, air emissions of lead from battery production are less than 1 percent of total U.S. emissions. The main sources of human lead exposure are from lead paint, gasoline, pottery, water pipes, and solder.

New developments that extend the life of traditional lead batteries three-fold are providing even greater environmental advantages. The large-scale deployment of hybrid electric vehicles brings significant fuel economy and emissions savings along with more power and a smaller footprint. As the technology advances, hybrid electric vehicles are becoming increasingly affordable for consumers.

BCI by the Numbers:

- BCI serves more than 200-member companies worldwide, representing every facet of the industry.
- Its automotive lead-acid battery recycling and safe handling legislation model has been adopted by 37 state legislatures
- BCI aspires to reach a 100 percent lead battery recycling rate.
- Since 1990, BCI has been producing a monthly report of industrial battery and charger sales.
- BCI provides industry standards for testing, dimensions, and sizes of lead-acid batteries worth more than $1 billion in the North American market each year.

Rewarding Progress

Innovation in lead batteries is continuing rapidly as the industry adapts to changing energy storage markets. BCI strives to stimulate this progress throughout the industry. The latest technical innovations in lead batteries are used in applications ranging from micro- and mild-hybrid vehicles to renewable energy storage and motive and traction power. Lead batteries remain the most popular rechargeable battery worldwide due to their unique combination of performance, low cost, safety, and recycling record.

A number of companies are collaborating with the U.S. Department of Energy's Argonne National Laboratory in Batavia, Illinois, to use its analytic technologies to accelerate research in the sector. Others are introducing new systems and next-generation batteries to boost production, improve performance and achieve consistent savings in automotive and industrial energy storage applications.

The number one spot on Crain's Chicago Business 2016 list of the most innovative local companies was occupied by BCI member, Midtronics, Inc. The Willowbrook, Illinois, company had Chicago's highest-rated portfolio of patents granted in 2015, based on key criteria including uniqueness of the patented ideas and likelihood of investment to develop and maintain them. The Midtronics ranking was based largely on the strength of its patent for a battery management network that connects automotive battery testers and chargers to a cloud-based information and analytics platform. This technology allows dealerships and auto service shops to easily monitor and update their battery service tools and related programs. It also enables enterprise-wide information management for automotive original equipment manufacturers and service chains.

Dedication to discovery and invention is a common theme among BCI's members and the association. According to Thorsby, "Technology has significantly increased the demand for electricity in a mobile environment. This is good news for battery manufacturers. They are focused on new ways to build better batteries that last longer and capture and store greater energy. The industry is going through a reinvention to compete with lithium ion, which is lightweight and often less expensive."

In addition, advancements in robotics and modifications of manufacturing equipment are supporting the industry-wide effort to improve plant health and personal hygiene standards. Thorsby notes, "Lead blood-level limits and target levels for workers of battery manufacturers and battery recycling companies is a pressing topic. If lead never leaves the machine that it's in, then that means no lead dust particles."

In 2015, BCI created the Sally Breidegam Miksiewicz Innovation Award to annually honor an industry thought leader and recognize innovation in equipment, processes, services, and products. Sally Breidegam Miksiewicz, former CEO and vice chair of East Penn Manufacturing, challenged the industry to innovate and strive to make the lead battery better. She is noted for saying, "Innovation is the thing that gives you the opportunity. It's the promise of our future."

The innovation program was born out of a desire to recognize efforts by the lead battery industry to continue meeting the energy demands of the world and address environmental challenges. Submissions are judged by the following criteria:

- **Sustainability** – Provides environmental stewardship and/or innovative recyclability to help create a greener tomorrow.

- **Safety** – Provides product or process stability and the ability to be safely commercialized.
- **Cost** – Can be easily commercialized, provides cost-optimized advantages and serves as an affordable alternative to existing technologies and processes.
- **Performance** –Meets or exceeds the need for application and industry requirements.
- **Uniqueness** – Is the first of its kind to market, rarely used by other organizations, or otherwise is different from existing products.
- **Value** – Directly benefits the lead battery industry (e.g., material reduction or avoiding pollution)

In a promotional video about the competition, Thorsby states that innovation occurs every day in the lead battery industry. Ideas start as exchanges in hallways, on the factory floor or at conference tables. Questions posed by customers and coworkers also stimulate new development.

"BCI and its members are committed to staying ahead of the curve on battery technologies and the best solutions for managing and monitoring them," Thorsby says. The award is a vehicle to recognize these contributions and inform the public about members' accomplishments.

Big data also plays a role in how BCI encourages industry advancement. The association maintains a database that includes information on automotive battery production shipments at the manufacturer and inventory levels, enabling members to gauge their performance against those of the industry. It also provides members with annual reports, so companies can keep abreast of ever-changing channels of distribution. A monthly update on U.S. industrial battery and charger sales is another by-product.

BCI also provides industry value by establishing technical standards for battery manufacturing and promoting environmental, health and safety standards. Model battery recycling legislation encourages good stewardship at both the state and federal levels. Nearly 40 state legislatures have adopted BCI's model, which prohibits lead batteries from being placed in landfills or incinerated and imposes a mandatory take-back system at the point of sale. In this way, the association is contributing to a worldwide effort to increase the overall lead battery recycling rate to 100 percent.

In 2016, BCI ran a $1 million public health campaign to thwart legislation in California that could have negatively impacted the industry. "This effort will save our battery manufacturers $30 million in superfund cleanup fees," Thorsby says. "It was a complex project, but eventually the legislature used our version of the bill.

One of the challenges of representing more than 200-member companies is that not all organizations are on the same page when it comes to proposed legislation or policy. To address differences among its members, BCI established a procedure that allows companies to continue their engagement with the association even when they may oppose one or more of its policies.

Thorsby believes that "everyone is entitled to dissent. Members are required to let BCI know that they intend to dissent on a policy, and that triggers us to review the policy. If the policy remains as is, the dissenting company is then cut off from all association activities related to that policy."

To accommodate this process, meeting agendas are structured so that contentious issues appear at the end, and the dissenting companies can leave the conversation at that point. Dissenting organizations are not included in regulatory and legislative conversations they oppose, nor do they receive access to related scientific research conducted by the association.

"Our dissenting policy still allows these companies to stay engaged in the organization, but not to hurt our policy efforts," Thorsby explains.

What Association Executives Can Learn From BCI

1. Enable dissenters. Organizations have their own agendas and they may not always align with their association's public policies. Provide a mechanism to allow these individuals or companies to dissent from certain policies but still engage with the association. At the same time, ensure there are protections in place to safeguard the association's public policy efforts against the naysayers.

2. Recharge your members. Offer an innovation program that recognizes, rewards and encourages innovation. It will also serve as an effective public relations tool to educate consumers about the benefits of your industry and how it's anticipating the future.

3. Be your industry's data warehouse. Become an indispensable source of information for your customers with highly targeted compilations of data that provide value for each specific audience.

Food for Thought

- What strategies could your organization use to encourage innovation among the membership?
- Would your association benefit from an opt-out option for members who do not support certain legislative or policy decisions?
- Are there data that you could collect and analyze that would improve your members' ability to do business? If so, what are the opportunities and challenges for pursuing such an initiative?

* Mr. Thorsby recently retired from SmithBucklin and is now principal at Frontwheel Consulting.

CHAPTER 19: FLYING ABOVE THE HEALTH CARE FRAY

Featuring: Rob Miller, Senior Vice President of Business Development, Strategic Planning, and Operations, 340B Health

Overview

"Now, I have to tell you, it's an unbelievably complex subject. Nobody knew health care could be so complicated."

—President Donald Trump, February 27, 2017

340B Health operates in a sector that is fraught with controversy and uncertainty. Access to affordable health care has been a contentious political issue in the United States for decades. In 1992, however, Democrats and Republicans came together and passed the Veterans Health Care Act, which as a provision included the 340B program.

The organization partners with public and nonprofit hospitals in caring for the most vulnerable patients. 340B Health is the leading advocate and resource for providers across the United States who serve their communities through participation in the 340B drug pricing program. This legislation requires pharmaceutical manufacturers to enter into an agreement with the United States Secretary of Health and Human Services to provide discounts to safety-net institutions and other entities serving needy patients. Members include hospitals and other types of medical facilities whose patients are primarily low-income and who receive Medicaid and Medicare payments for serving the uninsured. These organizations provide specified outpatient pharmaceuticals at free or at drastically reduced rates to patients who meet the income requirements. Patients who are insured pay full price, with the margin going back into the system to fund a variety of health care programs serving the needy. No tax dollars are used to fund the 340B programs.

340B Health monitors, educates and advocates for drug pricing and other pharmacy matters affecting their members and ultimately the nation's poor and underserved populations. They also ensure that members are properly administering and complying with program legislation and are well represented to Congress. The organization is funded through dues, conferences, and program fees. Memberships are offered for institutions, corporate partners, or contract pharmacy affiliates, and individuals who are part of a member organization.

340B Health by the Numbers:

- $8.5 million annual revenue in 2016
- 1,300+ member institutions
- 29 employees

Over the last 25 years, while Congress and five presidential administrations have debated how to best meet the health care needs of United States citizens, 340B Health has been flying above the fray, working to support their constituents.

Advocacy is at the core of 340B Health's business. The organization strives to create the best possible regulatory environment for the hospitals and health care systems it serves so that they can provide low/no cost pharmaceuticals to the needy. Protecting its members' interests has put 340B at odds not only with representatives of the executive and legislative branches of the federal government but also with allied associations.

It is a risky environment in which to operate. 340B Health must explore scenarios that would create barriers to members fulfilling their missions and continuously educate and reassure them that together they can create a positive future regardless of which party is in the majority.

A Different Kind of Risk

Intrigued by the impact that technology could make on the operation of nonprofit organizations, Rob Miller left his job at the National Association of Broadcasters to become an entrepreneur. His credentials include starting and profiting from numerous companies, including the association management software company known as Abila.

In 2016, Rob decided to return to association work as a leader in Washington, D.C., during the ramp-up to the presidential elections. He joined 340B Health as senior vice president, business development, strategic planning and operations.

With more than 20 years of experience as an entrepreneur, Miller is not one to shy away from a challenge. Health care reform was on the agenda of every Republican candidate for president. Despite the uncertainty about the future of the 340B program, Miller decided to join the organization to see how he could help.

Miller is no stranger to politics. He earned his master's degree in public administration from American University and spent the earliest years of his career at the U.S. Environmental Protection Agency and the U.S. Office of Management and Budget. Coming to 340B Health ties together many aspects of his career thus far. Although he is early in his tenure at 340B Health, his previous experience, successes, and challenges give him a unique perspective.

Many association executives think they are trying to instill a sense of entrepreneurship in their organizations. But Miller believes that they are actually attempting to create an organization that is innovative and agile. From his perspective, entrepreneurship is more about the risk than rewards. "I think of an entrepreneur as someone who has to make payroll every two weeks. Their business grows only if they can win more accounts. They hope they can create enough momentum before they run out of cash. Most associations are not in that game."

"Associations can talk all day long about being entrepreneurial, but generally they're not," Miller says. They typically have a reliable revenue stream from dues income and stable acquisition and renewal rates. "Associations often can grow just by raising their dues rates—and it is not uncommon for the increase to be five percent annually. Entrepreneurs must continually make ends meet. Each year the revenue challenge starts again. This makes the stakes and pressure much higher."

It is not difficult to see why Miller, a dyed-in-the-wool risk-taker, was attracted to 340B Health. While the organization is stable financially, it operates in a volatile political environment in which change is programmed to occur at least every two to four years, if not more frequently through regulations approved by the U.S. Department of Health and Human Services or the Health Resources and Services Administration.

Miller's goal in this new role might be characterized as creating positive momentum. That is difficult given not only the political climate but the culture of associations as well. According to Miller, "Most everything works against creating momentum related to innovation—mission, governance, regulations, legal, brand reputation, etc." Miller understands that, under the best of conditions, it is difficult for associations to address risk in a positive and empowering manner. Standard tools, such as scenario building and contingency planning, are not common exercises for association volunteer and staff leaders.

Job No. 1 for Miller is to build the trust that will help provide a platform for change and innovation. He is grateful to be partnering with and learning from Chief Executive Officer Ted Slafsky, also a former entrepreneur. Slafsky has worked with 340B Health in some capacity from its inception and can take the long view while he empowers his executive team to leverage uncertainty to drive innovation in the organization today.

What Association Executives Can Learn From 340B Health

1. Monopolies kill innovation. Miller believes that whether or not associations hold a monopoly on service to an industry or profession, projecting that they do can lead to complacency. Association executives can fall prey to their own marketing messages, even when they are true. When you think about your association as 'the leading, the largest, the only,' it is human nature to relax and enjoy the view from the top. Try this exercise: look at a brochure or your website and insert the word 'today' at the end of every statement describing the impact or scope of your organization. 'Our organization is the premier association for what we do...today.' What would need to be true if 'tomorrow' was inserted instead of 'today?'

2. Create a sense of urgency. Miller believes when most associations CEOs talk about creating an entrepreneurial climate, they are really talking about fostering innovation. Changing the mindset of staff and volunteer leaders is the first step. The next step is envisioning a positive future for the organization that is more than staying the course. 340B Health is an advocate and resource for its providers. But what if the 340B program goes away? How might the association continue to support hospitals? How could the organization keep on serving

communities and making a difference in the quality of life of the disadvantaged? Spending time with the board reflecting on these statements and the opportunities they create is the path to a sustainable future.

3. Float new ideas early and see if they take hold. Accustomed to fully fleshing out new concepts to procure capital, Miller has learned to engage the association's executive team in conversations about ideas as they are being formulated. "I throw ideas out there before we validate their merit or even decide if it is a good idea. Normally I would have done more homework before telling people. But what I have learned is that they need time to think about how the initiative might relate to the mission, our culture or potential regulatory restrictions. It gives me an opportunity to develop a business case as they warm to the idea and own it, as opposed to spending too much time upfront and finding out there is legitimate reason we cannot proceed. Giving my colleagues a chance to embrace the new idea may actually result in faster adoption in the end."

4. Use consultants to help drive change in both front- and back-office operations. It may be your prerogative when joining an organization in an executive position to make wholesale changes. Miller advises weighing the risks and rewards of replacing staff. Certain individuals are ideal long-term employees even though they may not have the specialized skills needed for a initiative. Consultants allow an association with enough revenue—either from operating surplus or reserves—to supplement the team with unique talent. It is a good use of surplus funds to advance the organization. "The mentality of many associations is that reserves exist to perpetuate the life of the organization, rather than as a tool to energize and grow," Miller says. "The revenue just sits there and provides little value other than comfort." So why not put it to use?

Food for Thought

- Is your board receptive to new ideas? Could you do a better job of helping them take ownership?
- What qualities make your association entrepreneurial? How could you promote a more entrepreneurial culture among your board and your members?
- How does your organization manage risk and uncertainty? What could you do to better prepare for the unexpected?
- How could your association use consultants to enhance operations?

CHAPTER 20: SUMMARY

The interviews introduced you to a diverse group of association leaders. They are engaged in managing industries that represent a cross-section of our community. As their challenges and successes demonstrate, associations are facing a new reality. This environment is characterized by uncertainty and change. It is a volatile climate in which continuing to do business as usual presents considerable liabilities. Association 4.0 demands a new orientation.

All the leaders we interviewed shared these qualities:

- An agile mind
- Boundless curiosity
- Courage to adopt new ideas
- Willingness to change before change becomes inevitable
- Consideration for organizational success over individual agendas

These characteristics also define a culture of innovation. Leaders who embrace change are ready to address and adapt to the impact of disruption in the marketplace. Unfortunately, you can't do the heavy lifting alone. The most difficult step in the journey toward becoming an Association 4.0 organization is bringing all of the players—board, volunteers, and staff—along with you. Almost every interview in this book highlights the need to share a common vision.

Participants in .orgCommunity's Innovation Lab have been exploring how to integrate an innovative approach into the association landscape. In our quarterly brainstorming sessions with leaders of all stripes, we've been piloting the Learning Modules that follow. The goal is to help you and your board to evaluate your future with ruthless objectivity and develop the flexibility to change course when needed.

One important discovery we've made is that you can't arrive at the correct answers without asking the right questions. Association professionals often perceive themselves to be problem solvers. Not having solutions feels uncomfortable. But precious human and financial resources are wasted when they are pointed in the wrong direction. Exploring the question before diving into a rapid-fire response is critical. It stops the conversation and provides focus while people shift gears. It makes participants take a step back and think critically. And finally, it unleashes creativity and generates energy.

Making the leap to Association 4.0 will require you to become a seeker. You will need to ask all kinds of questions—including fundamental questions about your organization's purpose and operations. One of the first and most urgent issues at hand is:

- Does the definition of who you serve need to change? If so, how?
- Can you broaden your constituent base to be more inclusive?
- Can your organization grow internationally?
- Could you become more connected to allied professionals and industries or increase your cultural or generational diversity?
- Can you become engaged with your customer's customer?

There are myriad other options that leaders who are seeking to successfully navigate the future should explore. The following is just a short list:

- How do we connect and engage with potential "nontraditional" collaborators who can help us achieve our mission?
- How can a new way of thinking open doors that we haven't even knocked on in the past?
- If we really take the public part of our mission seriously, how would it change who we serve and how we serve?
- How can we meld the Millennial's innovative mindset with the Boomer's need for significance?
- How do associations need to change the way they serve?

Industry 4.0 is like an oncoming tornado. We don't know where devastation will strike. Some structures will be leveled, and others may be left untouched, but the impact will be felt across our sector. Customer services and products are certain to experience the brute force of this storm. There is already fierce competition in the marketplace from other businesses providing the same, similar or better offerings. Simultaneously, the definition of a customer is expanding. This crowded arena demands a reinvigorated approach to sales, service and engagement with your public. Demonstrating an intimate knowledge of your constituents' goals and preferences and an ability to provide customized experiences will be mandatory. The distinction between service and experience will blur. Both will be governed by responsiveness to the customers' preferences.

Governance, strategy, and operations will need to become more agile to keep pace with the speed of innovation and the variety of invention. These topics are not typically included on the board's agenda.

The reference materials, templates and process found at www.PostioningForSuccessBook.com are designed to help you view your organization from the Association 4.0 perspective. As you move through the exercises, you will discover options and ideas that didn't exist before. You'll explore how your organization's business model, governance structure, or leadership needs to change to adopt new initiatives. Most importantly, your team will be working together to arrive at agreed upon goals and strategies. As your leaders and members become accustomed to looking for the right questions, you will grow closer to finding the answers you need to keep traditions that serve you well, eliminate conditions that impede progress, seize opportunities and become an Association 4.0 organization.

This book is just the first step. Look to us for guidance and tools to help you break old patterns and introduce a forward-facing culture as we explore this uncharted territory together.

CHAPTER 21: THE FACILITATOR'S GUIDE

About This Facilitator's Guide

This Facilitator's Guide includes everything you need to examine, plan and develop a strategy to become an Association 4.0 organization. You do not need to have expertise in technology or strategy development, but some experience in human resources, ideation or facilitation will be helpful. This Facilitator's Guide, the templates and a process guide can be found on our website at www.PositioningForSuccessBook.com.

The guide includes:

- An overview of what it means to be an Association 4.0 organization
- Modules that can be conducted as workshops at your organization to help you plan and strategize to remain relevant and future focused
- Resources, such as videos and templates, to help you document your journey on becoming an Association 4.0 organization

Overview: What Does it Mean to be an Association 4.0 Organization?

A world in which everyone and everything is connected through a network of smart devices and sensors is fast approaching ... and in some cases, might already be here.

The Fourth Industrial Revolution—or what some people refer to as Industry 4.0 and the Internet of Things—is the convergence of the digital, physical and biological worlds that will influence the way associations work and the nature of the work they do.

The Fourth Industrial Revolution creates "Association 4.0." The Fourth Industrial Revolution is powered by digital innovations coming to maturity today and transforming every company across the globe.

Technology advancements in:

- Advanced robotics
- 3D printing
- Artificial intelligence
- Sensors
- Cloud computing
- Internet of Things
- Democracy of Devices
- Big data
- Software as service

The Fourth Industrial Revolution is happening now with:

- Digital transformation
- Autonomous devices
- Physical internet
- Cybersecurity
- Big data

The impact of the Fourth Industrial Revolution on associations means getting even closer to customers so that your organization is more familiar, more responsive and more personal. Associations need to mass-customize products and services, explore crowdsourcing of these products and services and take on the toughest of problems. The organization needs to digitize products, services and even their operations. You will need to harness your data and sell them. Your organization will need to accelerate globally and become an ecosystem. How is your organization prepared to thrive in the Association 4.0 world?

Module 1: Define Who We Serve, Trends Impacting Our Organization, How We Need to Change, and the Impact of Technologies.

Estimated Time: 90 to 120 minutes

Module Outcomes
- Understand the trends impacting our industry
- Define who we should be serving
- Understand how advanced technologies will disrupt our industry

Module 2: The Questions We Need to Ask

Estimated Time: 90 to 120 minutes

Module Outcomes
- Review the trends impacting our industry (results from Module 1)
- Understand how the Fourth Industrial Revolution is creating the need for Association 4.0
- How to ideate on the right questions we need to ask
- Develop list of questions to ask (staff, leadership, audiences)

Module 3: Finding the Right Answers

Estimated Time: 90 to 120 minutes for each session. (Three sessions.)

Module Outcomes
- Understand the changing expectations for customers/members

- Define business models to consider
- How the governance model needs to change
- How the CEO needs to change

To download copies of the templates and the process guide, please visit www.PositioningForSuccessBook.com

ACKNOWLEDGMENTS

We are extremely grateful to the following individuals for sharing their knowledge, experiences, opinions and time:

Irv Bomberger, Former Executive Director, American Orthopaedic Society for Sports Medicine

Jim Drinan, J.D., CEO, American Planning Association

Abe Eshkenazi, CSCP, CPA, CAE, President and CEO, American Production and Inventory Control Society (APICS)

H. Steven Lieber, CAE, Former President and CEO, Healthcare Information and Management Systems Society

Paul A. Markowski, CAE, CEO, American Association of Clinical Endocrinologists

David Martin,CAE, CEO, Society for Critical Care Medicine

Stephanie Mercado, CAE, Executive Director and CEO, National Association for Healthcare Quality

Stuart Meyer, Former CEO, National Barbecue & Grilling Association

Robert Miller, Senior Vice President, Business Development, Strategic Planning and Operations, 340B Health

Tom Morrison, CEO, Metal Treating Institute Management

Bernadette Patton, Former President & CEO, Human Resources Management Association of Chicago

Gail Rutkowski, Executive Director, National Shippers Strategic Transportation Council

David Schutt, Ph.D., CEO, SAE International

Gary Shapiro, CEO, Consumer Technology Association

Dawn Sweeney, CEO, National Restaurant Association and National Restaurant Association Educational Foundation

Mark Thorsby, Former CEO, Battery Council International

Robert A. Voltmann, President and CEO, Transportation Intermediaries Association

Steve Welch, Executive Vice President and CEO, American College of Chest Physicians

We thank the .orgCommunity Association 4.0 Innovation Lab participants for their thoughts on the future of their organizations and the association profession:

Nicki Augustyn, Senior Vice President of Education, American College of Chest Physicians

Dawn Briskey, CAE, Executive Consultant, .orgSource

Bill Bruce, Executive Director, American College of Occupational and Environmental Medicine

Rupa Brosseau, Senior Development Manager, Foundation for Anesthesia Education and Research

Tom Conway, MBA, CPA, CAE, Chief Financial Officer, American Association of Clinical Endocrinologists

Christine Eme, Executive Director, Eastern Association for the Surgery of Trauma

John Forbes, consultant to global health care organizations

Mark Lenhart, Donor Development Manager, Society of Critical Care Medicine

David Martin, CAE, CEO, Society for Critical Care Medicine

Stuart Meyer, Former CEO, National Barbecue & Grilling Association

Ron Moen, Jr, CIO, American College of Chest Physicians

Joanie Muench, CEO, 922 Inc.

Jennifer Pitts, Director of Products and Programs, National Association for Healthcare Quality

Debby Rice, .orgCommunity, Director of Strategic Relationships and Editor

Sharon Rice, Consultant, .orgSource

Kim Robinson, Owner, Frontline Association Management, Inc.

Jonathan Thatcher, Former Director of Research, APICS

Mark Thorsby, President, Front Wheel Consulting

Special thanks to **Sharon Rice**, who inspired and guided us in creating this book. Sharon was instrumental in interviewing several of the CEOs and challenging our thinking.

Sharon elevates the work of nonprofits and associations by creating strategies that ensure relevance and longevity while advancing their missions. Her specialties and experiences include nearly 10 years as vice president of strategy at APICS.

Sharon is an expert in board planning, leadership and workforce development, long-term business plan development, digital business transformation, product and service planning, international strategies, program development, complex project management, mergers and partnerships, education planning, research, content and publication planning. She now serves as an Executive Consultant with .orgSource and on the advisory team of .orgCommunity.